# What *Really* Happened in Colonial Times

## A Collection of Historical Biographies

Compiled by

### TERRI JOHNSON

Illustrated by

### DARLA DIXON

**BRAMLEY BOOKS**
*www.bramleybooks.com*

A Division of Knowledge Quest, Inc.
An Oregon Corporation

Published by BRAMLEY BOOKS
A Division of Knowledge Quest, Inc.
P.O. Box 789
Boring, OR 97009
www.knowledgequestmaps.com

Cover Design by Cathi Stevenson
Illustrations by Darla Dixon

Printed in the United States of America
Copyright © Terri Johnson, 2007
All rights reserved
ISBN # 1-932786-23-6

Publisher's Cataloging-in-Publication data

Johnson, Teresa Lynn.
       What really happened in colonial times : a collection of historical biographies / compiled  by Terri Johnson ; illustrated by Darla Dixon (What really happened... series, v.3).
       p. cm.
       ISBN 1-932786-23-6
       Contents:  Pocahontas - Maiden of Peace -- My Grandmother, the Martyr - Lady Alicia Lisle -- James Cook - Explorer of the South Seas -- Rachel Walker Revere - the Ride of her Life -- Admiral Lord Nelson - Victory! -- Catherine Ferguson - Really, Really Free! -- Lucretia Mott - Equality for All -- Narcissa Whitman - A Seed in Fertile Soil.

1. United States--History--Colonial period, ca. 1600-1775--Biography. 2. America--Discovery and exploration. 3. Women--United States--Biography. 4. United States--History--Revolution, 1775-1783--Biography. 5. Slaves--United States--Biography. 6. Frontier and pioneer life--West (U.S.)--Biography. I. Dixon, Darla. II. Title.

E187.5 .J64 2007
920--dc22                                                   2007904499

## Contributing Authors:

### Karla Akins
*Catherine Ferguson - Really, Really Free!*

### Andrew Boynton and Tracey Boynton
*Lord Admiral Nelson - Victory!*

### Linda Ann Crosby
*Rachel Walker Revere - The Ride of Her Life*

### Jennaya Dunlap
*Pocahontas - Maiden of Peace*
*Narcissa Whitman - A Seed in Fertile Soil*

### Judith Geary
*Lucretia Mott - Equality for All*

### Jocelyn James
*James Cook - Explorer of the South Seas*

### Virginia Youmans
*My Grandmother, the Martyr - Lady Alicia Lisle*

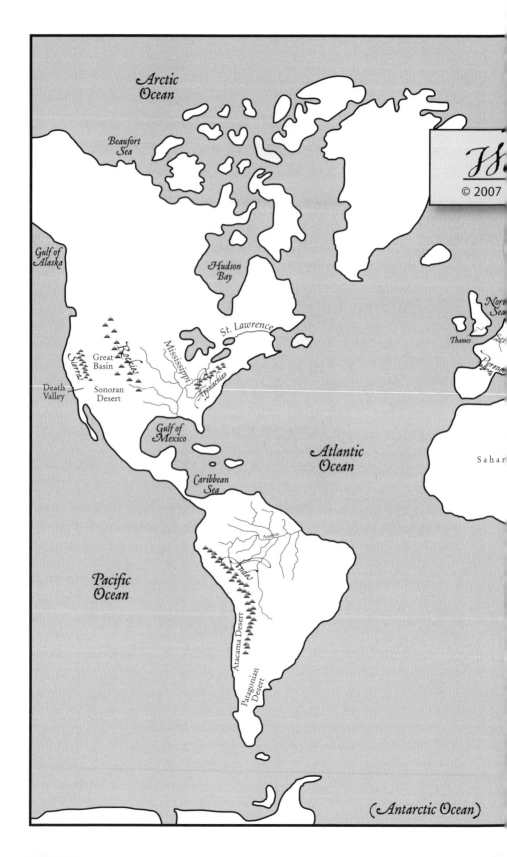

Arctic
Ocean

Beaufort
Sea

Gulf of
Alaska

Hudson
Bay

St. Lawrence

Rockies

Mississippi

Appalachian

Sierra

Great
Basin

Death
Valley

Sonoran
Desert

Gulf of
Mexico

Caribbean
Sea

Atlantic
Ocean

North
Sea

Thames

Pyrenees

Sahar

© 2007

Amazon

Andes

Pacific
Ocean

Atacama Desert

Patagonian
Desert

(Antarctic Ocean)

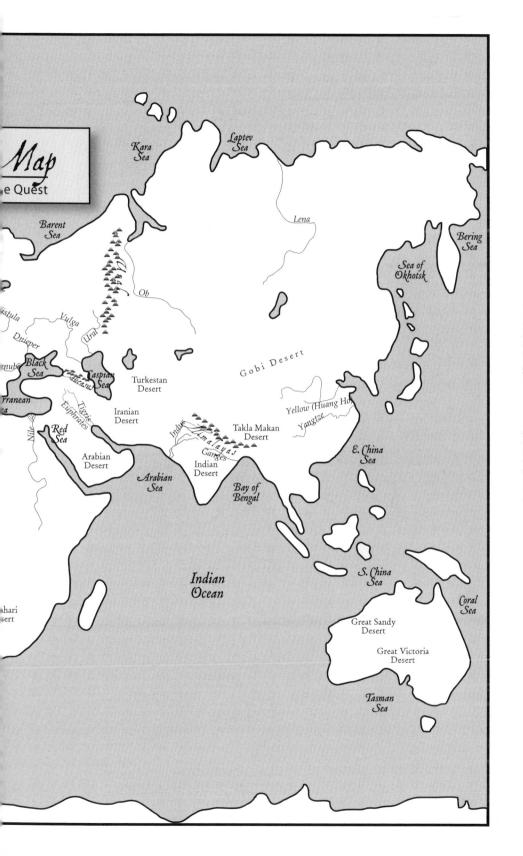

*Other books in this series:*

What *Really* Happened in Ancient Times
What *Really* Happened During the Middle Ages
What *Really* Happened in Modern Times
*(scheduled for Spring, 2008)*


*e-books also available at*
*www.bramleybooks.com*

# TABLE OF CONTENTS

*"We hold these truths to be self-evident, that all men are created equal, that they are endowed by their Creator with certain unalienable Rights, that among these are Life, Liberty and the pursuit of Happiness."*

**Declaration of Independence, 1776**

*"So in everything, do to others what you would have them do to you, for this sums up the Law and the Prophets."*

**Matthew 7:12**, NIV

# A Word from the Publisher:

Dear reader, young and old alike,

History is an interesting blend of facts, legends, assumptions and speculations. Historical research uncovers events from the past – how, when and where an incident happened. It cannot, however, fully explain motivations – why someone did what they did – or how an event can be interpreted so differently by two or more eye-witnesses. History is the story of people from the past – people who lived and died based on their convictions and perceptions about the world they lived in. *What Really Happened in Colonial Times* is a compilation of stories based upon actual historical happenings as found in various historical writings. The authors have been careful not to add to nor subtract from the actual events of history. We have, however, added small fictional elements, or daily life details, as to contribute to the flow of the biographies and the ease of reading. In the same way, some unsavory details have been left out or glossed over for the benefit of our younger readers and listeners. We hope that you will enjoy these historical tales of real life people and learn something new about the time period when the world was being colonized.

*Terri Johnson*

*To my mother for her courage, love and perseverance, raising five children from a wheelchair in spite of pain, illness, and discouragement, persevering through the greatest storms and the worst hardships to be there for us, encouraging us to do what we loved and pursue our dreams, and helping us all along the way, sharing in our joys and sorrows. And for her compassion and love toward anyone suffering or in need, and her courage in standing up for the rights of those who-face unjust prejudices and bigotry.*

# Pocahontas

## Maiden of Peace

### 1595 – 1617

*by Jennaya Dunlap*

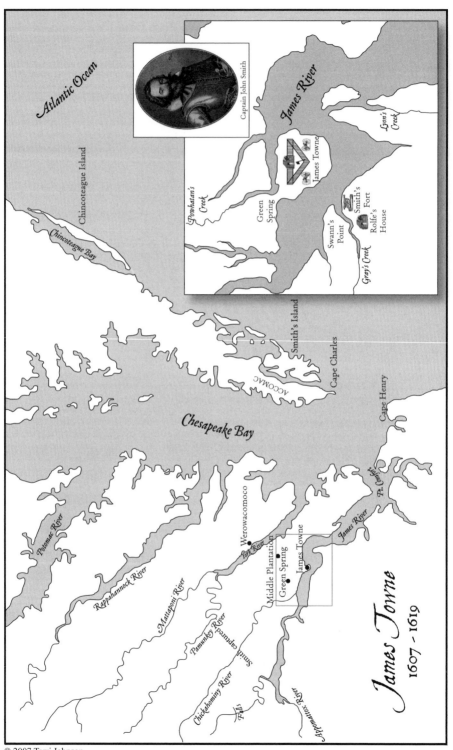

Atlantic Ocean

James River

Captain John Smith

Lyon's Creek

Powhatan's Creek

Green Spring

James Towne

Smith's Fort

Rolfe's House

Swann's Point

Gray's Creek

Chincoteague Island

Chincoteague Bay

Smith's Island

Cape Charles

ACCOMAC

Cape Henry

Chesapeake Bay

Potomac River

Rappahannock River

Mattaponi River

Pamunkey River

Chickahominy River

Falls

Appomattox River

Smith Captured

Werowacomoco

Pipe Creek

Middle Plantation

Green Spring

James Towne

James River

Pt. Comfort

*James Towne*

*1607 - 1619*

© 2007 Terri Johnson

# I

# Pocahontas

## Maiden of Peace

*by Jennaya Dunlap*

1607, Werowocomoco, Virginia

The crowds inside the longhouse pressed close together, whispering with great excitement. The heat in the dark room grew stifling from the mass of people, but Pocahontas was used to it—such was always the case during occasions of great significance.

She stood straight and poised by her mother's side, her pale deerskin dress decorated with painted shells and a blue fringe across the front. Her father, Powhatan, the great chief of the Algonquin tribe of the same name, was stretched out in regal repose on a seat of furs, his uplifted gaze roaming the room. His numerous wives were gathered around him, his favorites seated close by, while the others were clustered farther away.

"Bring the prisoner in," Powhatan commanded, raising one arm toward the wide doorway. Immediately the crowds stepped back toward the walls, clearing a path across the room.

A group of young braves near Pocahontas whooped, keeping up a steady drumbeat. Two strong men, experienced in war and armed with tomahawks, appeared in the doorway with a man such as Pocahontas had never seen before grasped between them. His skin was white, like her frock, and his eyes, lighted by the sun outside, were as blue as the waters of the Great River. His hair was pale too and he was covered in heavy-looking garments.

At his entrance a wild, warlike shout went up through the room. The white man was led toward Powhatan's throne of furs. His step was calm, but when he passed Pocahontas his eyes met hers for a moment and she saw fear in them. And for good reason. She shuddered, knowing all too well what would probably happen tonight.

Powhatan's favorite wife presented the prisoner with a bowl of water and a bunch of feathers to wash and dry his hands. Powhatan motioned for him to sit down, and all around him the men sat cross-legged on the bare ground. The women brought in food—turkey and smoked deer meat with vegetables.

The men ate in silence, their portions no bigger than those of the white man. When the meal was finished, the braves pulled the prisoner to his feet and turned him to face Powhatan. The village spirit men crowded around him, their faces painted black and menacing.

An older man, an advisor from a nearby tribe, stepped forward, his eyes narrowed at the prisoner. "This man was trespassing on our land, taking our food without our permission. And when we tried to capture him, he shot two of our men with a magic bow."

The spirit men let out blood-curdling whoops. "Let him die!"

The white man stepped forward, his gaze meeting Powhatan's. "It is true that I killed two of his men. But they killed two or three of my companions and tried to kill me, so the loss is equal on both sides. Please, good sir, spare my life—I have no wish to cause harm to your people."

The spirit men and advisors bent over Powhatan and spoke to him in low tones. Pocahontas held her breath, tension building inside her. When the men stepped aside, she scanned her father's face. With a sinking heart she could see what his decision was even before he spoke.

"The white man must die," he commanded, raising his eyes just once to look at the prisoner. The spirit men let out an eerie cry of triumph, while the drumming of the braves grew loud and ominous. Several strong men rolled in two big boulders, laying them to rest at the foot of Powhatan's throne.

Suddenly Pocahontas couldn't stand it any longer. She pushed her way through the crowd toward Powhatan. The other women stepped aside to make room for her to pass. Surely my father will listen to me, his favorite daughter!

She felt the glares of the spirit men as she came to his side, but she spoke in a clear voice. "Please, father—don't shed any more blood. This man came to our land because he was hungry, and he promises not to do any more harm."

A combination of amusement and hesitation showed on Powhatan's face, but before he could answer, one of the spirit men leapt forward with a shrill, angry shout.

"The War God demands the sacrifice of this man's life. If he is spared, the spirits will bring evil on us and demand more sacrifices from among our people." The sound of his voice sent shivers down Pocahontas' back.

Powhatan lifted his chin and raised his arm toward the braves in a gesture for them to continue. In a rush, they grabbed the white man and forced his head against one of the boulders. Pocahontas fell back, not wanting to see what would follow and yet unable to turn away. Her heart leapt with adrenaline, and she shivered with tension.

The braves raised their clubs, ready to strike his head. "No!" With a cry, Pocahontas sprang forward and threw herself across the white man, covering his head with her own. She closed her eyes, waiting for the death that must surely come—listening to the shocked gasps of the women.

But nothing happened. The room settled into silence, and she heard her father's voice. "Rise up, my daughter. The white man will live."

Her heart still pounding, Pocahontas pulled herself to her feet. Trembling, she looked at her father, but his eyes held the amusement she had seen earlier, not the anger she was afraid of.

"My daughter has chosen for you to live," Powhatan announced, rising to his feet. "Go in peace." When Pocahontas turned toward the white man, he was smiling.

The next day, as she walked with him among the oval-shaped houses of Werowocomoco, she learned that his name was Captain John Smith. He was one of the leaders of a village up the river, a place called Jamestown.

"It was a brave thing that you did," he continued. "Today your father is willing for our peoples to live together in peace. He has asked for gifts from Jamestown, and in return he has promised me my safety."

Pocahontas nodded, remembering the talk she had had with her father the night before, pleading with him not to harm the white men. This morning he had called John Smith to a council in the longhouse and made the arrangements he had just mentioned.

He was lucky, she knew, for her father didn't often heed her requests for mercy. When he was angry, his punishments were great and vindictive. Those who fell out of his favor often were beaten severely or put to death, in the way John Smith had nearly experienced.

John Smith had told her much of his life and the ways of the white men who had landed on the shores of the Great Sea. He had led a rebellious life, running away from home at the age of 16 to fight in Henry IV's war against the Spaniards and later, against the Ottoman Empire. In 1602, he was captured and sold as a slave to the Turks, but later escaped.

Two years later, he joined the voyage to the New World to colonize Virginia. "I made trouble on the voyage," he admitted, looking out across the river. "In fact, Captain Newport was going to have me executed upon our arrival, but they discovered my name in the sealed list of the new leaders, and my life was spared."

"So last night was the second time," Pocahontas turned to him with curiosity.

"Aye, the second time," John Smith still had a faraway look in his eyes. "And now I must get back to my men before they think I really am dead."

*January, 1608*

A few weeks later, Captain John Smith returned to Jamestown, rested and loaded with provisions. Powhatan sent several braves with him to collect the gifts he had promised, along with Pocahontas and one of her older brothers. Even before they reached the hastily-built wall of high wooden slabs that surrounded the town, several men, pale-skinned and well-dressed like John Smith, emerged from the gate and rushed toward them.

Pocahontas could see from their faces that something was wrong.

They shouted to John Smith as they approached, gesturing in agitated excitement. Pocahontas couldn't understand the language they spoke, but John Smith's guide translated many of their words into her native Algonquin tongue.

"Come quick—most of the men are leaving!" One of them pointed toward a ship looming at the water's edge. It was huge, unlike the simple canoes of Pocahontas' people, with numerous sails of pale canvas flapping in the wind. Men were carrying crates and bundles on board.

"Where? Back to England?" John Smith stood still, his brow knit with a heavy frown. "But it's the middle of winter!"

"They say they'd rather endure the voyage than continue to die of starvation here," another man replied. "They won't listen to reason— the council has tried everything." John Smith turned toward the coast, his steps hurried, and the others followed him.

"Five more died while you were away," said a heavy-set man with graying hair who had joined them. He had an air of authority about him. "Only thirty-eight are left of the original one hundred and five settlers, and our provisions are running out."

Pausing on the swampy ground that led down to the waters, John Smith took aside the man who had just spoken and they conferred in low tones. The ship had just begun to pull away from the shore when he straightened up and turned to give his command.

"William, get the men together and point one of the cannons toward the ship. Send someone out to give the mutineers this warning— if they don't turn back, the Discovery will be blown out of the water."

For several tense moments, Pocahontas was sure a battle would ensue, especially when she saw the angry glares of some of the men toward John Smith. But the three men on the boat he had sent to give

18

the warning returned with the news that they had decided to stay.

When the crisis was over, John Smith led the way toward the fort. "And now to show you the power of the big guns," he announced. Turning to one of the cannons facing outward from the walls, he ordered his men to load it and fire it at an old tree that was stiff and frozen with thick icicles.

Pocahontas braced for the sound of the cannon, but when it came, it was far louder than she had imagined. The braves fell to the ground, but she had been leaning against the wall and she only jumped.

"My father will be well-pleased," she told John Smith when she stopped shaking.

But when they surrounded the cannon to move it to their boats, they discovered it wouldn't budge. After several efforts, they had to give up, though Pocahontas knew her father would be unhappy. Instead, they filled the boat with the other gifts John Smith offered.

As Pocahontas returned to the fort, she heard angry voices once again. She reached the gates in time to see John Smith dragged between two men, toward one of the thatch-roofed wooden huts inside. A swarm of others gathered around, shouting in accusing tones.

"What is happening?" Pocahontas begged of the guide.

"He is being tried by the council—they accuse him of causing the deaths of the men who went with him on the expedition," the interpreter told her before hurrying to talk to some of the bystanders.

Pocahontas and her brothers pressed close, watching closely for further signs of what was happening. John Smith was no longer in sight—he had been brought inside the house and the door shut behind him. After what Pocahontas guessed by the sun's position was an hour, the interpreter reappeared with a grave look.

"They have sentenced him to be executed," he said simply. The door opened behind him and John Smith was led out amid the chaos of the gathered men. Before Pocahontas could speak, he had passed, with little more than a desperate look in her direction.

A feeling of helpless horror passed over her. This was the third time he faced death—and this time she couldn't save him. She turned away as two men lowered a rope from the building, the noose ready.

Then a shout went up through the street, followed by the call of a horn. Pocahontas followed the colonists to the gate. She gasped in surprise—another great ship stood next to the one the colonists had tried to escape in. Painted on the black side were the words John and Francis.

Perhaps forty men disembarked, and one of them was greeted with the respect of a leader. Pocahontas overheard them calling him "Captain Newport." As he approached the fort, John Smith hurried out to meet him, unharmed. Desperate to know what was going on, Pocahontas looked for the interpreter.

"Captain Newport has brought fresh men and many supplies," he explained when she found him.

"But what of John Smith? What will they do with him?" Pocahontas asked.

"He is saved—Captain Newport overturned the order to execute him," the interpreter answered.

That evening, a celebration was held onboard the John and Francis, and Pocahontas found that she and the other Indians who had come with her were guests of honor. The next day, she and the others returned home with their canoes well-loaded.

Because of the swampy ground and the colonists' disinterest in hard work and lack of farming knowledge, their crops had failed,

Pocahontas

leaving them with little for the long, freezing winter that had taken hold. Knowing her new friends would starve without help, Pocahontas convinced her father to allow her and a group of women to bring food—corn, meat, and other supplies—to Jamestown every week or so.

She was shocked by her first trip back, for she found most of the settlement in a blackened, smoking rubble. Flames had burst out in the night a few weeks earlier, getting out of control before the colonists could stop the fire. Now even the remaining supplies from Captain Newport's ship were gone.

She found Captain Smith giving instructions to some of the men, his face grave. But when he saw Pocahontas and the food she had brought, he reacted with joy. The Jamestown colonists gave her royal treatment, urging her to stay overnight at the fort. The next day, she spent the afternoon playing with the English boys outside the fort walls. They ran and jumped, and Pocahontas showed them how to turn cartwheels on their hands.

In February that year, Captain Newport and Captain John Smith arrived on the shores beside Werowocomoco, their boats laden with valuable merchandise from England to trade in return for furs and food. Pocahontas and the other villagers watched in awe as the colonists carried an English bed—complete with blankets and what John Smith called a "mattress"— to the longhouse for Powhatan.

Powhatan refused it, reminding them that it wouldn't fit through the doorway of his hut. "We want guns and swords in exchange for our corn, not the strange luxuries of the white men."

John Smith and Captain Newport put their heads together, talking rapidly in anxious tones. Pocahontas knew they were worried that Powhatan would use the weapons on the colony. Stepping forward, John Smith settled the matter by convincing Powhatan of the rarity and value of the shiny, blue beads he had brought. After negotiations, her father agreed to the trade.

Thomas, one of the boys Pocahontas had met on her last trip to Jamestown, was with them this time. When Powhatan was introduced to him, he sat up on his throne of furs and called John Smith forward to make a proposal.

"Let this son of your people, Thomas, stay among us and learn the ways of my tribe," he suggested, his chin raised in an imperial manner. "In return, Namontack, the son of my favorite wife, shall go to live in Jamestown and learn your language. Thus the two would know the ways of both peoples, and help to interpret better between us."

Pocahontas turned to glance at John Smith's face—she could see that he liked the plan. He bowed in respect and signaled his approval. When the colonists' ship left for Jamestown, Pocahontas' half-brother stood on the deck, waving to her and her siblings. Behind her, Thomas stood on the shore, ready to take his place among her people.

Thomas and Namontack learned quickly, opening the way to bring mutual respect and good communication between the two peoples. But both sides had their own greed—the colonists for land and wealth, and Powhatan for power and weapons to control his enemies. The short-sighted goals of each group brought many clashes.

As summer approached, Powhatan, still angry that John Smith hadn't delivered the promised cannons and guns, sent seven braves to sneak into Jamestown by night and seize as many English swords as they could find. But they were spotted by the watchman and an alarm was raised. Within days, Namontack arrived in Werowocomoco to report that the men had been taken prisoner and were in the Jamestown guardhouse.

Pocahontas was surprised when her brother came to fetch

her, telling her Powhatan wanted to speak with her. After much consideration, he had decided to send her to Jamestown to negotiate for the men's release.

When she arrived at the fort, her friends greeted her warmly, as usual, but this time she went straight to John Smith to carry out her mission. She found him in one of the storehouses, directing some other men. He stepped outside with her, telling her he had just been elected the president of the Jamestown council.

Pocahontas was relieved to hear it—her job would be much easier with him in charge. After a long talk and some hesitation on John Smith's part, he finally agreed to release the prisoners, on the condition that they would promise to stay away from Jamestown.

The next day, Pocahontas was on her way home with the freed warriors. Her people greeted her with cheers, carrying her to the longhouse on their shoulders.

In part because of Pocahontas' influence, relations between the Virginia tribes and the colonists remained on good footing for a while. But, slowly, more and more white people arrived and began to build settlements. The bang of their shotguns in the woods where they hunted became a common sound. Land the Indians felt they had a right to was taken without payment.

Pocahontas sensed that her people were losing patience. She could feel their silent hostility growing, and she saw the darkening of her father's brow as he listened to reports of the colonists' success. But she could only wait and watch, continuing to live her life between two cultures, with deep ties to both.

As autumn came, with the rich gold and red hues of the trees, and the energetic preparations of the animals for the chill of winter, things had gotten worse. Pocahontas had heard her father and other chiefs talk of going on the warpath, so she was surprised when she discovered that Powhatan had invited the white men up the river to camp near Werowocomoco for a few days. Something didn't seem right.

Leaving the night's meal of deer and fish to cook under the watchful eye of Alawa, one of her half-sisters, Pocahontas sprinted toward the longhouse. In the distance she could hear the voices of John Smith's men as they set up a shelter by the river. She paused outside the dark doorway, her heart pounding. Before she entered, however, she heard her father's voice, low and ominous.

"We'll wait until they've gone to sleep and are unguarded," Powhatan was saying. "Then you and several other warriors can sneak in and kill them."

"What if they suspect something?" It was the voice of her oldest half-brother.

"We must act friendly until the moment of the ambush," Powhatan replied. "Perhaps we can send Pocahontas and some other women to their camp with food."

Chills ran down Pocahontas' back, and she turned to run, trembling. So her father's plan was to kill them while they were most vulnerable. The sudden realization came that John Smith and her other friends would die tonight unless she did something to save them. But how? Certainly her father wouldn't change his mind. She thought quickly and decided what she must do.

When Alawa came with Powhatan's order for them to prepare the food for the visitors, she took her aside and gave her quick instructions. Before long, they were on their way to the finished wooden and canvas shelter where John Smith and his men were seated around a fire.

Pocahontas could see that her presence had the effect Powhatan was hoping for—the men let down their guard, assuming all was well. Alawa did as she had requested, taking the other women with her to leave her alone with John Smith. Knowing she had only a few moments, she blurted out her warning, urging him to set up sentries to keep watch through the night.

It took a while to convince him, but when she did, John Smith responded with emotion, pouring out words of gratitude. "You have saved my life a second time. How can I repay you? If you stay, I can reward your kindness with gifts from the treasure we brought with us."

Pocahontas shook her head. "I cannot stay—my father will be angry enough as it is." She slipped away, tiptoeing in the darkness until she reached her tent, where she burrowed under the bearskin blanket beside Alawa. The danger was not over yet—she could feel tension in the air.

She woke the next morning to the whispered sound of Alawa's voice beside her. In the half-light she could barely see the outline of her face, bent over her. "Are they—are the men safe?" Pocahontas held her breath, waiting for the answer.

"They kept their watch all night, and the warriors didn't dare to attack," Alawa replied softly. "But oh, Matoaka, our father suspects who did it, and his anger is great against you." Indeed, from that day on, Powhatan was cold and distant toward her, hardly speaking to her.

1609

Pocahontas stood still on the shore of the river with one of her small half-brothers, barely older than a papoose, in her arms. The colonists' boat was back, and already the messengers from Jamestown were on the shore. Her brothers hurried to meet them, their moccasin-

26

covered feet making little noise in the leaves.

The messengers stopped to talk to them, and even from a distance Pocahontas could see her brothers' faces darken. With a sinking heart, Pocahontas handed the boy-child to one of the other women and ran toward them.

"What has happened?" she begged of her brothers as they passed her on trail, on their way back to the longhouse.

"The white captain, John Smith, was killed by one of their big guns," one of her brothers turned to speak to her while the other hurried on. She could see in his eyes that he understood the fear and horror she felt at the news.

"No—it couldn't be," Pocahontas' heart was heavy in her chest as she turned to the white men. "Is it really true?"

The men shuffled their feet, their guns hanging limply at their sides. They nodded, and a bearded man she had met once before at Jamestown stepped forward. "It was an accident with gunpowder. Terrible—we only heard of it last night."

Shaken with horror and disbelief, Pocahontas turned and fled, past the gathered colonists and past the people of her village. The trees passed like blurs of brown and green, and the river to one side seemed to roar with a warning of trouble. She ran until the village was far behind, sinking to her knees beneath an old chestnut that hung over the rushing waters.

Today she couldn't even see her reflection in the angry waters. She leaned back against the tree's trunk, staring at the sky. Her heart ached, for she knew what would happen without John Smith to solve the quarrels and disputes between their people. War could not be long in coming—more bloodshed on both sides.

And she was right. Captain Ratcliffe, who replaced John Smith in the leadership of Jamestown, didn't make the same efforts to keep good relations between the colonists and the Powhatan Indians. Constant fighting broke out between them, with unreasonable demands and much violence from both sides.

Later that year, Captain Ratcliffe sailed upriver to Werowocomoco, as John Smith had done before, and found himself in an ambush. He was captured and tortured to death, and the last vestiges of the fragile peace were broken.

Pocahontas grew weary of the wailing war cries and nightly drumming of the braves and the spirit men, and the scalping and bloodshed nearly every day. Fear pounded inside her when she lay inside her tent with her sisters, hearing the bangs of the colonists' guns and the taking of prisoners. She was pained, too, by her father's unwillingness to communicate with her, and by his cold distance because of her friendship with the white people.

When he called her to the longhouse and sent her to travel with some others to a nearby tribe further up the Great Potomac River, she was relieved to go and leave the horrors of war behind for a time. They would be trading furs, corn, and tools made of copper.

Japazeus, the chief of the tribe, and Kanti, his beautiful young wife, welcomed Pocahontas into their home, happy to extend hospitality to the favorite daughter of the great Powhatan Chief. When they asked her to stay with them awhile, Pocahontas accepted gladly, because she was not eager to return to the scene of so much violence.

She was now about eighteen years old. As things grew worse between her people and the growing numbers of colonists settling in Virginia, she worried about her own family as well as those she had come to know and love in Jamestown. Reports from Jamestown were grave.

The winter of 1609 had brought disease and starvation, leaving only 60 survivors. They were on the point of abandoning the fort when supply ships arrived from England, along with a new governor.

One day, in spring of 1613, a great ship appeared on the shore of the Potomac tribe, with the huge banner of England waving in the wind. Japazeus greeted the white man who disembarked like a brother, and introduced him as his good friend, Captain Argall. There was something in his eyes that Pocahontas didn't like, though he seemed friendly enough.

With Japazeus to translate, she showered him with questions about her people and about her friends at Jamestown.

"Things are bad, very bad," the captain furrowed his brows as he spoke. "Neither side is willing to make peace." Then he looked at Pocahontas with a frown and asked some rapid questions to Japazeus in English. In the conversation that followed between them, she heard her own name used several times.

She gave Japazeus a puzzled look. "What is he saying about me?"

"He's just surprised to find you here," was all he would say, and quickly he led the captain to his spacious wigwam, where Kanti was preparing a meal of fish and corn.

A few days later, Pocahontas was seated cross-legged in her favorite low tree branch outside the wigwam, stringing shells she had gathered into a delicate necklace. Kanti told her Captain Argall was leaving and asked her to go with Japazeus and her to see him off at his ship.

Pocahontas slipped down from her perch and followed, glad to make her friend happy. When they reached the river, where the ship

29

loomed tall and strong, she stopped to stare at the sails as big as the whales her people used to hunt, fascinated. Kanti asked to go aboard, telling Pocahontas she was eager to see the inside of the ship.

"I'll wait here—I've already seen inside some of the ships at Jamestown," Pocahontas told her with a smile.

"If you don't come, then I can't go either," Kanti protested with a glance at Japazeus. "I would be uncomfortable without another woman with me." Pocahontas hesitated, uneasy this time.

"Please come with us—for Kanti's sake," Japazeus begged.

Pocahontas didn't want to disappoint Kanti, so at last she assented to go aboard. Captain Argall looked relieved, and quickly ushered his guests onto the great ship. He led them into a long room, where a table was set with dishes that shined like silver.

"Be seated—I have a feast prepared for you," he beamed, pulling out chairs for them. Pocahontas couldn't help wondering how he had gotten the food ready so soon—and how he had known to have the table already set with four places. But she placed those thoughts behind her and enjoyed the deer meat, fruit and vegetables, and the bread made of corn.

By the time the meal was over, they had agreed to spend the night on Captain Argall's ship and return to shore in the morning. The captain led Pocahontas through a narrow hall to a wide room lined with windows, where guns and cannons were lined up facing outward. He assured her that Japazeus and Kanti would be along soon—they only wanted to talk to him privately for a few minutes.

Pocahontas hunched in a corner and tried to stay awake, but she fell asleep before Japazeus and Kanti came. When she awoke, the gunroom was dark except for the bluish glow of dawn, and strangely silent. Something felt wrong—Pocahontas sat up in a sudden panic. A quick glance around the room told her Japazeus and Kanti weren't there.

Holding back the fear that swelled in her throat, she slipped out of the gunroom, and ran without a sound through the hall. Hearing voices on the deck, she opened the door leading there, and stood still, unnoticed by Captain Argall and her two friends. They were near the railing, and even in the predawn darkness she could see the silvery glint of a copper kettle the captain passed to Japazeus.

Pocahontas strained to hear what he said, and realized with surprise that he was speaking in her own tongue. "Thank you for help," he told Japazeus and Kanti.

Anxious to leave the ship, Pocahontas made her presence known and rushed toward her friends. "I want to leave—right away. Please, take me back to the shore." The startled expression on Japazeus' face turned to a guilty look, alarming her even more. Pocahontas turned to Kanti and saw that her arms were full of gifts of copper and other metals.

"My adopted brother, Japazeus, and his wife may leave the ship, but you must stay," Captain Argall stood behind her, blocking her from fleeing.

"Why? Where are you taking me?" Pocahontas turned frantically to call for Japazeus, but he and Kanti had disappeared. With a rush of fear and agony, she realized it had all been a plot—her friends had betrayed her!

"The other leaders and I have decided to keep you as a hostage, in hopes of convincing Powhatan to hand over the men he has taken prisoner." Captain Argall was leading her away from the deck. "Don't worry—I won't hurt you. You'll be released as soon as your father fulfills our demands."

In moments, she found herself back in the gunroom. She fell to the ground, weeping, as the ship began to move. The shore grew distant, and the trees became only specks at the river's edge. How could this be happening? Pocahontas watched from the window, her eyes blinded with tears.

When her first grief was over, she decided to make the best of her situation. If her capture would help to make peace between her people and the colonists, she told herself, then it would be worth it. Still, she couldn't help wondering how her father would react when he heard the news.

Her keen knowledge of the river helped her to get her bearings, and soon she realized they were on their way to Jamestown. The ship docked there, and Captain Argall sent a messenger to Werowocomoco with the news of her capture, along with his demand that Powhatan give up the prisoners and stolen goods.

Pocahontas waited anxiously for her father's response, but it was three months before he replied. Perhaps he didn't worry about what the colonists would do to her, she reasoned to herself, but it still hurt. He agreed to give up some of the goods, but not all, and none of the prisoners.

Captain Argall replied that Pocahontas would be kept hostage until the rest of his demands were fulfilled. The wait this time stretched into months, then nearly a year. In the meantime, Pocahontas was brought to Henrico, a new settlement further down the river from Jamestown.

There, it would have been easy for her to escape, but she was happy in the home of an English minister, Alexander Whitaker, and his wife, who treated her with kindness and hospitality. Her mind was quick, and her memory good, so she picked up the English language quickly, learning to read and write as well.

Mr. Whitaker read to her from the Bible and taught her about Christianity. She learned eagerly, and soon she wanted to become a Christian. When she was baptized, Mr. Whitaker asked her to choose a new name, and she asked to be called Rebecca, after the wife of Isaac in the Bible.

A young man named John Rolf often visited her at the Whitaker house. He had lost his young wife and child when his ship sunk near Bermuda, and now he owned a tobacco plantation near Henrico. He became fond of Pocahontas, and wrote to Sir Thomas Dale, the governor of the Virginia colonies, to ask his permission to possibly marry her.

In March of 1614, Sir Thomas Dale took her back onboard Captain Argall's ship, and she was taken to the shore of the Pamunkey River, near her homeland. But the ship was not alone—several other ships had sailed with hers, along with 150 armed men.

Pocahontas wept when she heard the news of Thomas Dale's plan. He had sent a message to her tribe, telling them to either surrender the rest of the goods and prisoners or fight for her. Pocahontas knew it would result in only one thing—violence and terrible bloodshed.

And she was right. The Indians responded by attacking with bows and arrows, and the English soldiers raced ashore to retaliate, burning forty villages and killing many of the Powhatan people. After days of war, two of Pocahontas' brothers asked to see her. They were brought onboard, and she greeted them joyously with embraces. Her hope returned when they promised to urge Powhatan to make peace and obtain her freedom.

John Rolf and another man went ashore to negotiate with Powhatan, but found him absent. His brother, Apachamo, greeted them instead, and they found him wary of the endless war. He, too, agreed to push for a truce, and the ships returned to Henrico.

A month after the standoff, when she had been taken back to Henrico, John Rolf asked for her hand in marriage. She accepted, and word of their engagement spread quickly. Her father, whom she hadn't seen for almost two years, sent word of his consent through an old uncle of hers, Opachisco. On April 5, 1614, her wedding day, her two brothers arrived in Henrico, bearing gifts for the wedding.

The small Henrico church was decorated with bouquets of spring wildflowers, fresh from the fields. A crowd of her friends, both colonists and Indians, gathered for the celebration, seated together peacefully after so much war. Looking resplendent in her white gown, Pocahontas entered on Opachisco's arm.

Cheers erupted in the church as she took the hand of her husband. Their marriage, a Native American Algonquin maiden to a white colonist from England, brought a new bond of peace between the two peoples and cultures she loved.

*Epilogue*

After their wedding, Pocahontas and John Rolf lived at Varina Farms, John's plantation across the river from Henrico. In 1615, their son, Thomas, was born, and baptized with both English and Algonquin names.

A year later, the men in charge of the Virginia Colony asked Pocahontas and her husband to travel to England, in hopes of attracting more colonists with her now-famous story. To Pocahontas, it would be her chance to see the land across the ocean that she had heard so much about.

When Powhatan heard the news of their upcoming trip, he sent eleven men from the tribe to accompany the couple and their small child, along with some of Pocahontas' women friends. Tomocomo, the head spirit man, was among them, at Powhatan's command carrying a stick on which to make notches to count the people of England.

The party arrived in the port of Plymouth, England in June, 1616. Tomocomo started his task of census taking, but soon gave up after he encountered London's busy streets. He then set about to fulfill another of Powhatan's orders—to find John Smith, in spite of the colonists' claim that he was dead. To Pocahontas' shock, she discovered that indeed he was alive, and living in London.

He did not offer to see her, but he sent a letter to Queen Anne, urging that she be shown respect and given royal treatment, lest the natives in the New World should turn against the colonists if they heard a bad report. On January 5, 1617, she and Tomocomo were presented to King James at a banquet in Whitehall palace.

Pocahontas enjoyed the sights of London, going to plays and meeting English leaders, but the pollution and smoke-filled air made her sick, and she had to move to the suburb of Brantford. It was there that John Smith paid her and Rolf a visit, at a social gathering.

In March of the same year, she and John Rolf, along with their son, embarked on the voyage back to Virginia. Before they had gotten further then Gravesend, along the River Thames, Pocahontas became severely ill with pneumonia, induced by London's bad air, and she had to leave the ship. Even with a doctor's care, however, she soon succumbed and, in her weakened state, died. She was buried in Gravesend, England, far from her native land. John Rolf returned to Virginia with the sad news, arriving sometime in 1617.

In later years, John Rolf lost his good reputation due to involvement in corruption, but Pocahontas never lived to see his fall from honor. Thomas Rolf, who also was sickly, was left in London in the care of Sir Lewis Stuckley, where he remained until the age of 20.

When he arrived in Virginia in 1635, he discovered that his father and his Grandfather Powhatan were dead. However, he had not been forgotten, for both had left him large tracts of land and great wealth. The peace Pocahontas had helped establish lasted years after her death, and became the legacy for which her short but fruitful life was remembered.

*About the author:*

Jennaya Rose Dunlap wrote this story at the age of 17. Jennaya is homeschooled and the editor of a magazine for home schooled girls, ages 8 to 18, Roses In God's Garden, published by LightHome Ministries, www.lighthome.net. She is also the author of Against All Odds, a historical novel set in World War II Poland under Nazi occupation, published as a serial  story in her magazine. Jennaya enjoys writing and researching, drawing, singing and horseback riding. She enjoys spending time with her family on their acre beside a meadow with a mountain view, in California. She graduated from high school this year and plans to continue writing to publish.

*I thank the Lord for all His good gifts.*

*I thank my family for their unwavering support:*
*my mother, my sister and my brother, my six children, and my*
*wonderful husband.*

*And I thank my sixth-grade teacher, Joanne Heiserman Shaffer, who*
*encouraged me to get an education and strive for excellence.*

My Grandmother, the Martyr

# Lady Alicia Lisle

## 1614 - 1685

*by Virginia Swarr Youmans*

Outer Hebrides

*England*
1685

Aberdeen

SCOTLAND

Dundee

*North Sea*

Inner Hebrides

Glasgow

Edinburgh

Ellingham

Newcastle on Tyne

*Yorkshire*

Bradford

Isle of Man

Manchester • Sheffield
Liverpool

Nottingham

WALES • Birmingham

ENGLAND

Stratford Upon Avon
Cardiff
Oxford Cambridge

*Thames*

Sedgemoor London
*Wiltshire*
Taunton Winchester
*Hampshire*
Southampton Portsmouth

Plymouth

Isle of Wight

Isle of Purbeck

*English Channel*

# II

## My Grandmother, the Martyr

# Lady Alicia Lisle

*by Virginia Swarr Youmans*

This is the journal of Joshua Whitaker, grandson of Lady Alicia Beconsawe Lisle (1614-1685), describing the last days of my grandmother's life. (The journal itself is fictional, but the characters and events within it are based on actual events.)

*July 26, A.D. 1685*

My name is Master Joshua Whitaker of Grindleton, Yorkshire, England, and I will be ten years of age this 22nd of December next. I am the son of the Reverend Robert Hugh Whitaker of Yorkshire and Margaret Lisle Whitaker of Hampshire. I have set about to write this journal to make a record of the life of my dear grandmother, the Lady Alicia Beconsawe Lisle, who has been arrested and imprisoned this very day for the crime of harboring traitors – enemies of King James II.

My mother and her sisters, my aunts Mary, Anne, and Tryphena, are of course quite distraught about the whole situation. Father tries to comfort Mother, reminding her that Grandmother is over seventy years old and that surely the judge will take her age and her charitable works into consideration. But Mother cries and says that none of that matters because Grandmother is the widow of a regicide!

I had never heard that word before, so I set about to discover what it means. According to my Latin lessons, *regi-* is the root of the word for "king," and *-cide* is a suffix that means "to kill." So a regicide is someone who has killed a king! That could explain why I never have heard much at all about my grandfather, Lord John Lisle, who died more than ten years before I was born. I suppose that until now I never was very much interested in such things. Since Father, Mother, and the aunts are too upset to answer questions right now, I shall have to visit with some of the older servants and find out something of my family history.

*July 27, A.D. 1685*

This morning after we broke our fast I offered to help Old Bess, Grandmother's housekeeper, to carry the dishes from the breakfast room to the kitchen to be washed. She seemed rather surprised by my offer but grateful for the help, since these days there are not as many servants to do the work of keeping a large house in operation. I so enjoy staying here at Moyle's Court, which is my grandmother's ancestral home at Ellingham, near the village of Ringwood. While we were working, Old Bess told me that Grandmother came back here to live at Moyle's Court after my grandfather died in 1664. She also said that her title of Lady Lisle was now just a courtesy, since Cromwell's titles have been revoked since the Restoration, and that Grandmother really should just be called Mistress Lisle or Dame Alice. Then Old Bess looked around, as if to make certain that no one else could hear, and she told me that Lord John, my grandfather, had been assassinated in Switzerland by an Irish Royalist!

42

"Your grandfather had to take wing to Switzerland after the fall of the Commonwealth and the Restoration of King Charles the Second in the year 1660," whispered Old Bess. "He had been Lord Chief Justice under Oliver Cromwell. He was the one who drew up the sentence which condemned King Charles the First to be put to death in the year 1649, although they say he did not sign it himself. And Lord John administered the oath of office when Cromwell was made Lord Protector!"

Well! You can imagine how surprised I was to learn all of this exciting information about my own grandsire! And it is no wonder that no one speaks of these things in such troubled times as these. The current king, James II, is the younger brother of Charles II, who died only this past February. I do not suppose King James is very much inclined to be friends with the family of the man who brought about his father's death, especially since he is a Roman Catholic and we are Nonconformists. So that is why Grandfather is called a regicide! And why my mother fears that my grandmother's trial may not go well for her. From the fear in Old Bess's eyes and the tears on her face, I see that she, too, worries about my grandmother's fate.

*July 30, A.D. 1685*

As we all wait to hear what will become of Grandmother, my parents are too distracted to pay much attention to me or my brothers and sisters. We are happy to be here at Moyle's Court, where my mother and all her sisters and brothers grew up together. Many of them are here now, consoling each other, the aunts crying, the uncles pacing up and down the floor, dispatching messengers to Grandmother's influential friends in London to seek their support. Grandmother herself is imprisoned somewhere, I know not where, awaiting trial. I hope I shall soon get the chance to go and visit her.

I take this time to write of the events leading up to this week. Although I have not always paid very close attention to politics and religion, the two favorite topics of this family, I was aware of the recent Battle of Sedgemoor, which took place to the west of here more than a fortnight ago. I remember my parents talking about a battle – a rebellion, they called it – and I recall that their tone was one of disapproval and regret that it had occurred. They mentioned a person named the Duke of Monmouth, who had led the rebels against the king's soldiers, and my mother had cried and said, "It is happening all over again, Robert, just as it did in the time of my father." And Father had comforted her and said, "No, my dear Margaret, it isn't that bad, surely. King James is not such a terrible ruler, and most of the people are content to have him as their king. Things will soon settle down, you will see."

But then we learned of the horrible vengeance that was brought against the people of the western region for their part in the rebellion, especially in Taunton. Colonel Kirke and his men gathered up suspected rebels and took them into captivity. And then, instead of carrying them off to London for trial, Colonel Kirke turned the signpost of the White Hart Inn, which he made his headquarters, into a gallows, and he began to hang them without trial! I learned most of this from our servants, since my parents did not want me to hear about such bloody acts. But I heard my mother appeal to my father in despair, "Are these the deeds of Christian soldiers? Will God allow such tyrants to go unpunished?" And my father had put out his hand both to calm her and silence her, warning her, "Be careful of what you say, my dear. Even the walls have ears." And I knew he meant that even one of our servants could betray us by a word to the wrong person.

Eventually we heard that the Duke of Monmouth had been captured and beheaded for his part in the rebellion. I remember thinking it was rather a hard way to die, but I supposed he knew the risks he was taking when he decided to fight against the king. My grandmother had once told me that the Stuart kings all believed in something called the Divine Right of Kings. She explained that it meant that the king had a God-given right to rule. King Charles I had believed in it so strongly that he once sent home all the members of Parliament and ruled without them for eleven years. I asked Grandmother if she believed in the Divine Right of Kings, and she had smiled in a strange way and said, "Thy will be done. Thy Kingdom come on earth as it is in heaven." And I do not think she was talking to me anymore.

*August 2, A.D. 1685*

Today I gained further information about my grandmother and the crimes with which she is charged. I followed Old Bess around while she did her work this afternoon, and she was happy to tell me all about Grandmother's childhood and youth, much of which were spent here in Moyle's Court. (Old Bess grew up here, too, since her father was the gardener in those days, and she and Grandmother were playmates as children.) Grandmother's father was Sir White Beconsawe of the Isle of Wight, and her mother was Edith Bond of the Isle of Purbeck. Old Bess continued on with the family genealogy, talking about Sir White's father, William Beconsawe, and his mother, Alice White, which explains where he got his strange name and where Grandmother got hers. But then I began to grow confused with Old Bess's ramblings about this Lord Hungerford and that Lady Berkeley, so I tried to steer her to more interesting subjects by asking her some pointed questions.

"Old Bess, what did Grandmother do to get her into trouble

with the king?" I asked. "Why would they imprison an old lady simply for giving shelter to someone for the night?"

"Oh, my lad, you do not understand the times," Old Bess said mournfully. "These were not just simple vagrants that stayed the night at Moyle's Court. My lady had been in London for the first week of July, and only came lately home to Ellingham. Doubtless she knew of the Battle of Sedgemoor on the sixth, but when Mr. Hickes sent Mr. Dunne with a message on the twentieth to ask her leave to stay here for the night, she allowed it because she thought his only trouble was being a Nonconformist preacher. She knew that sheltering such a man would not bring a charge of treason. She knew not that he and his companion, Mr. Nelthorpe, had just fought for the Duke of Monmouth against the king in the Battle of Sedgemoor! Someone else knew, though, and he told Colonel Penruddock, who arrived the next day with a troop of soldiers. Oh, my poor lady! Poor Dame Alice! How many times she sheltered Catholic Royalists when they were hiding from Lord Cromwell's men! And this is how they serve her!"

And here Old Bess lapsed into sobbing and praying, rocking back and forth in her chair. I felt dreadful for the pain I was causing her, so I ceased my questioning, patted her shoulder, and left her alone for a while. Now I shall go in search of Edward, the stable master, to see if he can tell me anything more about the Battle of Sedgemoor or the Duke of Monmouth.

*August 3, A.D. 1685*

After my last entry, I went looking for Edward and found him in the stables, giving orders to his stable boys about caring for the horses and cleaning out the stalls. When he finished with this work, he accompanied me outside to lean against the fence and watch some of the horses romping in the meadow. I asked him what he knew about the Duke of Monmouth and the Battle of Sedgemoor. He looked alarmed, and he gazed around from side to side, as if to judge whether anyone were watching or listening, just as Old Bess had done that first day.

"My boy," he told me quietly, "you'd best be forgettin' about such things as these. Can only come to more trouble."

"But, Edward," I protested, "how am I to learn the truth and keep from danger if no one will tell me? I need to know what has happened!"

Edward sighed, then began to speak. "I'll tell you, but you must promise me not to go about asking anyone else about such things. Promise me!"

I nodded and promised, so he continued to tell me. "A long time ago, just about the same time that Prince Charles became King Charles the Second, he had a son named James. But the boy's mother was not the queen. No, the king was just a young man then, and not yet married to Queen Catherine. This was his 'natural' son."

I must have looked confused – I had no idea what he was talking about – so he tried to explain it better. "He was illegitimate – born out of wedlock. So everyone knew he could never become king," Edward said. "While he was still a very young man, his father gave him the title of 'Duke of Monmouth.' Later he became captain-general of the army, and he married a rich heiress. He would have had a fine life if he had been content with his lot. But there were many around him who hated the king's brother James, who is now our sovereign. They knew that James was a Catholic, and they feared that if he took the throne when King Charles died, all those who were not Catholic would be persecuted, just as they were in the time of Bloody Queen Mary." Edward shuddered at the thought. "They wanted Monmouth to claim the throne of his father, to take it from his uncle, King James."

I asked, "So what happened to the duke?"

Edward shook his head. "He was banished, twice, but then he returned just last month, ready to raise an army of citizens against the king's soldiers. But those who had pretended to be his friends were wrong about the people's love for him. Oh, yes, some of the people fought with Monmouth, especially in the west. But most didn't want any part of another civil war. When Monmouth's army of farmers and townsmen met the king's men at Sedgemoor on the sixth of July, they were defeated, and Monmouth was soon captured. Although he tried to talk his way out of it, King James showed no mercy. Monmouth was beheaded on the fifteenth of July."

I cannot believe it. First, that this Duke of Monmouth had the audacity to challenge his uncle the king, and second, that King James had put to death his own nephew! What does this mean for my grandmother, who is *not* a relation of King James? Will he have mercy on an old lady?

*August 5, A.D. 1685*

This morning I asked my father what has become of my grandmother's steward, Carpenter, since I just realized that I had not seen him since we arrived here after Grandmother's arrest. I never liked Carpenter very much, so I did not miss him. He was old and tall and thin, and he never smiled, certainly not at any of us children. But I was surprised by my father's response.

"Carpenter is gone, Joshua. He is not wanted here anymore."

"But, why, Father? What has he done?" I could see by his face that it was something very grave indeed. "Oh, Father, surely it was not Carpenter who told Colonel Penruddock about Grandmother's visitors!"

48

Now it was Father's turn to be surprised. "How do you know about Colonel Penruddock?" he asked. Then he said, "Never mind. But do you know the whole story about Colonel Penruddock?" I shook my head, certain that I did not. So Father continued.

"First of all, no, Carpenter was not the one who told the colonel about your grandmother's visitors. That was a man called Barter. But when the colonel and his troops arrived, Carpenter was so frightened that he quickly told all he knew and even led the soldiers to where Mr. Hicks and Mr. Dunne were hiding in the malt house. He probably would have given up Mr. Nelthorp, as well, but he knew not where he hid." I must have made a face, because Father quickly warned me, "Don't judge Carpenter too harshly, my boy. It is a dangerous business to cross an officer of the king's army. We do not know how we would react if we were in such a situation."

Father continued his story. "About thirty years ago Colonel Penruddock's father led an uprising in Wiltshire against the Commonwealth. Your grandfather, John Lisle, was Lord Chief Justice at the time, and he sentenced him to death. Doubtless Colonel Penruddock, who would probably have been just a youth at the time, has not forgotten and now sees his opportunity to avenge his father's death on the family of his executioner."

"But, Father," I protested, "surely he does not blame an old lady for something that her dead husband did thirty years ago!"

Father looked grave. "I fear he makes no distinction between them," he said. "Your grandfather made many enemies, and since they cannot punish him, some of them are now closing in on your grandmother in his place. Such is often the way with evil men."

"Then I will take vengeance on their families!" I vowed fiercely. But this only made my father look sad.

49

Lady Alicia

"No, Joshua. 'Vengeance is mine, saith the Lord.' It is not ours to take," he said. "Better to follow your Grandmother Alice's example and show mercy to all people, rich or poor, Nonconformist or Roman Catholic."

"But, Father," I protested again, "look how that behavior has served Grandmother! She is being punished because she gave shelter to those men."

"Yes, Joshua, and when she faces the Lord on the Day of Judgment, she will hear Him say, 'Well done, good and faithful servant.' Now, please do not worry about it anymore. The Lord is still sovereign. May His will be done."

*August 13, A.D. 1685*

A few days ago my mother received word that she was permitted to go and visit with Grandmother, and I pleaded with her to allow me to go along as well. She frowned in thought as she looked at me and considered whether or not she should allow me, and then she smiled sadly.

"I suppose you should spend as much time with her as you are able," she said. "Our time with her may be short." Father protested this last comment, but she put up her hand and shook her head. "Besides, Joshua can help with the baby."

We were to take my youngest brother Daniel along as well, since he was only two years old and therefore not yet weaned. I was to help with Daniel's care and amusement. A carriage transported Mother, Father, Daniel, and me from Moyle's Court northeastward across the countryside past Southampton to Winchester, where Grandmother is being held at the Eclipse Inn until her trial. Since the journey was one of over twenty miles, Father had elected to stop for the night at an inn just north of Southampton and continue on to Winchester the next morning.

When we arrived in Winchester we went immediately to the Eclipse Inn. We will be staying here, too, during our visit. It is a large, clean, busy place, much better than the dark and dirty rooms of last night. I do not know what I expected when I met with Grandmother for the first time since her arrest, but I was somewhat surprised to find her quite unaltered. She was sitting in a rocking chair by the unlit fireplace in her room, where Mother threw herself down at her feet and broke out into quiet weeping. Grandmother looked mildly surprised to see this person crying in her lap, and then she gently brushed back Mother's hair and made soothing sounds. Father went over to Grandmother and bent down to kiss her silver head, and I waited in the doorway, holding Danny by the hand.

"Joshua, my dear boy, come to me!" Grandmother exclaimed, and she reached out her arms to hug me. Then Danny climbed up onto her lap, and she smiled with real contentment as she leaned back to hold him and rock him. "It is so good of all of you to come visit me," she said. "How I have missed you all!"

We spent a few more minutes with her, and then Father asked me to take Danny to our rooms for his nap. He assured me that I will have time to speak with her later.

*August 25, A.D. 1685*

I have not written in this journal for many days because I have been helping with the care of Daniel and spending as much time as possible with Grandmother. Most forenoons I take Danny over to Grandmother's rooms, where she likes to hold him on her lap while she tells me about her childhood and youth. I shall have to begin another journal to record all the wonderful stories about castles and estates, kings and queens, knights and villains, lords and ladies, and the sovereign God who rules over all of us and directs our paths.

Grandmother has received many cards and letters from well-wishers who are praying for her and appealing to the king and his council for mercy on her behalf. Mother says many of these people were sheltered by Grandmother in much the same way she sheltered those Monmouth men. Some of the people she helped were Roundheads fleeing King Charles I, and some were Cavaliers hiding from Oliver Cromwell's men. Although she is a member of the Reformed faith, she believes in showing God's love to all who need help, be they Catholic, Anglican, or Puritan.

Her face changes slightly when I ask about my grandfather, Lord Lisle. Although she tries not to show it, I can see that she disapproved of his actions towards King Charles I in 1649 and the trouble it brought to our family after the Restoration in 1660. She refuses to speak much of that time. I was surprised to learn, however, that she was Lord Lisle's second wife, his first wife having been Mary Elizabeth Hubbard, who died in 1633. When Grandmother married him in 1636, she was only 22, and he was a 36-year-old widower with six children! They went on to have more children together, including my mother.

My favorite times with Grandmother these past weeks have been watching her smile as she smooths Danny's hair and thinks back to her days as a young wife and mother. If my calculations are correct, she would have been only eight years older than Uncle William, Grandfather's eldest son, when she became his stepmother. When I pointed that out to her, she actually laughed out loud.

"Yes, you are right, Joshua," she said. "And William made sure I knew it, too!"

I also enjoyed listening to Grandmother read the Scriptures to

Danny and me, and giving us our catechism lessons, although I tell her that I doubt if Danny has any notion of what he's saying.

"It is not necessary to completely understand God's ways to know that they are true and good, to commit them to memory, and to make them your own," she said slowly, looking at me closely. "Can you explain the trinity? Eternity? Infinity?"

I shook my head. "Not entirely," I replied.

"Precisely," she shot back. "But you know they exist, don't you?" I nodded. "You keep reading your Bible and practicing your catechism," she told me, "and someday, when you're in a hard spot – although I pray the Lord never puts you in a spot as hard as this one I am in – the Lord will bring those truths from His Word to your mind, and you will find comfort in them."

I know that Grandmother is right, for I can see the comfort that she derives from the vast amount of Scripture that she has committed to memory. I pray that God helps me to do the same.

*August 27, A.D. 1685*

Today was the day of the trial at Winchester Castle, but I was not allowed to attend. I had to stay here at our rooms at the Eclipse, looking after Danny and wondering what is happening to Grandmother. I had hoped the trial would be cut short once the judge heard the ridiculous charges against a sweet old lady, but I began to fear that, since it went on all day, it did not bode well for my grandmother.

Later this evening, when everyone returned to our rooms at the inn, I knew right away that the trial had not gone well. Grandmother seemed very tired and aged, and Mother's eyes were red with weeping. Father gently helped Grandmother to her room, under the close watch of the guard, while Grandmother's younger sister, Lady Elizabeth Tipping, hurried to assist her and get her some refreshment. I took Mother's arm and guided her to a chair in the sitting room, for I could see that she was near collapse. Danny was asleep in the bedroom.

"Oh, Joshua, it was terrible," she moaned. "Judge Jeffreys ranted and raged at everyone who tried to speak for your grandmother, and he practically told the witnesses for the prosecution what to say. When it was your grandmother's turn to speak, he tried to browbeat her as well, but she remained calm and unwavering." She sighed as she removed her bonnet. "How she can stay so calm amidst such turmoil can only be the very presence of the Holy Spirit, comforting her and carrying her through this. She even dozed off a few times. But that judge must be possessed by a demon!" And then she began to weep again.

I was glad to see Father returning from Grandmother's room. His face was lined with care and fatigue as well, and he sighed heavily as he sat down next to Mother.

"Is the trial ended, Father? Is there a verdict?" I asked anxiously.

"Yes, my son, it is ended. Your grandmother has been charged with harboring traitors to the Crown, although no traitors have as yet been tried or convicted, and there is no evidence that she knew they were traitors when she gave them shelter. In spite of Judge Jeffreys' blatant attempts to influence the jury, they were reluctant to convict her. But in the end he had his way, and they finally issued a guilty verdict. The sentence will be given tomorrow morning." Father shook his head and stared into the fire. "I cannot believe the Lord has let this go so far."

I asked him softly, hoping Mother would not hear, "But surely the sentence will be a light one for such an old woman?"

Father looked at me forlornly. "I think not, Joshua," he said. "Harboring traitors is a capital crime, punishable by death."

I will spend this whole night in prayer for my grandmother, and I am sure my parents will as well. May the Lord have mercy on her soul.

*August 28, A.D. 1685*

Grandmother's sentence was handed down this morning. She is to be burned at the stake, which is the usual way for women convicted of treason. When the judge pronounced this penalty, Mother fainted into Father's arms. But Grandmother sat quietly and bowed her head. I don't think she even cried. The sentence was to be carried out immediately this afternoon, but, after the church leaders of Winchester protested, Judge Jeffreys did finally relent and grant a reprieve until the 2nd of September. I am so numb that I cannot cry or do anything. Has God forsaken His faithful servant?

*August 31, A.D. 1685*

Our friends in London have been successful in submitting a petition to King James II to have mercy upon Grandmother. Today we learned that the king has ruled that the execution still stands, but instead of being burned at the stake Grandmother is to be beheaded. Her body and head will be turned over to the family for burial. I had hoped King James would dismiss the charges altogether, but my parents and aunts and uncles say that he intends to let Judge Jeffreys have his way and to make an example of her. Nevertheless, we are at least grateful to God that her death will be swift and painless and that her body will not be drawn and quartered or her head put upon a pike for all to see.

Great-Aunt Elizabeth is allowed to sleep in Grandmother's room, so at least she will have the comfort of a loved one for her last night on earth.

*September 2, A.D. 1685*

My grandmother, the Lady Alicia Beconsawe Lisle, was put to
death by beheading this afternoon in the marketplace at Winchester. I
am thankful that I had the chance to kiss her goodbye and receive her
blessing in her room at the Eclipse this morning. And I know that I
shall see her again in heaven, where we both shall "glorify God and enjoy
Him forever," as we confess in the Shorter Catechism. She went to the
scaffold with a serene expression on her face, and, although I am sure her
step faltered now and then, her faith in God never did. May the Lord
grant us all such a faith!

*September 12, A.D. 1685*

The family was permitted to bring Grandmother's remains home,
and a few days later we held a funeral and burial at St. Mary's Church in
Ellingham. Father says a special stone will be erected to mark her grave.
He gave me a paper which contained a copy of Grandmother's statement
that she read in her own defense at the end of her trial. It comforts me to
know that she could forgive her enemies – for enemies they surely were
– and go to meet God, the Supreme Judge, with a clean heart. I copy
some of it below:

"Gentlemen, Friends and Neighbors,

"I die in expectation of pardon of my sins, and acceptation
with the Father, by the imputed righteousness of Jesus Christ: He
being the end of the law for righteousness to every one that believeth. I
thank God, thro' Christ Jesus, I depart under the blood of sprinkling,
that speaketh better things than that of Abel; God having made this
chastisement an ordinance to my soul. I did as little expect to come to
this place on this occasion, as any person in this nation; therefore let all
learn not to be high-minded, but fear. The Lord is a Sovereign, and will

take what way He seeth best to glorify Himself by His poor creatures; I therefore humbly desire to submit to His will, praying of Him, that in patience I may possess my soul.

"...But I forgive all persons that have wrong'd me; and I desire that God will do so likewise. I forgive Colonel Penruddock, altho' he told me he could have taken those men before they came to my House. I acknowledge His Majesty's favor in revoking my sentence; and I pray God he may long reign in peace, and that the true religion may flourish under him...and return humble thanks to God, and the reverend clergy that assisted me in my imprisonment."

It is simply signed, "Alicia Lisle."

May she rest in peace.

*Epilogue:*

In 1688 King James II's second wife, Mary of Modena, gave birth to a male heir who would be raised Catholic, which once again divided the English people. That same year William of Orange, nephew and son-in-law of the king, was invited by seven leading English statesmen to come to England to take the throne. King James II and his family were forced to flee to France. William's wife Mary, James's daughter from his first wife, Anne Hyde, would rule jointly with him. This is sometimes called the Glorious Revolution or the Bloodless Revolution. One of the first acts of parliament under William and Mary was to reverse the ruling against Alice Lisle on the grounds that the prosecution of her trial had not been properly done and that the guilty verdict had been forced by "the menaces and violences and other illegal practices" of Judge Jeffreys. Many consider her death a "judicial murder," and her story is included in some older versions of Foxe's *Book of Martyrs*. Some

Whitaker genealogists believe that this Joshua Whitaker, son of Robert and Margaret Lisle, is the Joshua Whitaker who went on to become a Quaker, a member of the Society of Friends. He made arrangements to settle with his wife and children in Pennsylvania, that haven of religious freedom established by William Penn, but he died, according to some sources, in a battle on the Isle of Man in 1719 at the age of 43. His wife Jane Parker Whitaker and their children emigrated to the New World and settled in Pennsylvania, New Jersey, and North Carolina.

*About the author:*

Virginia (Ginny) Swarr Youmans, 44, is a native of Lancaster County, Pennsylvania. She is the wife of Sergio Youmans and the mother of André, Emilio, Olivia, Cassandra, Magdalena and Lorenzo, who are all taught at home on their family's farm in southern Tennessee. Ginny is a freelance editor and author, and she holds a B.S. in secondary education (English) from Millersville University of Pennsylvania, with concentrations in linguistics and ESL. She is a member of Hopewell Presbyterian Church (ARP). A genealogy buff, she enjoys using history, literature and her family tree to make education interesting for her children. If her ancestor Joshua Whitaker was the grandson of this story, then Lady Alicia Beconsawe Lisle was her 9th great-grandmother.

*For my husband - I couldn't do this without you
and for my boys, whose adventurous spirit is undimmed.*

*Soli Deo Gloria*

# James Cook

Explorer of the South Seas

1728 - 1779

*by Jocelyn James*

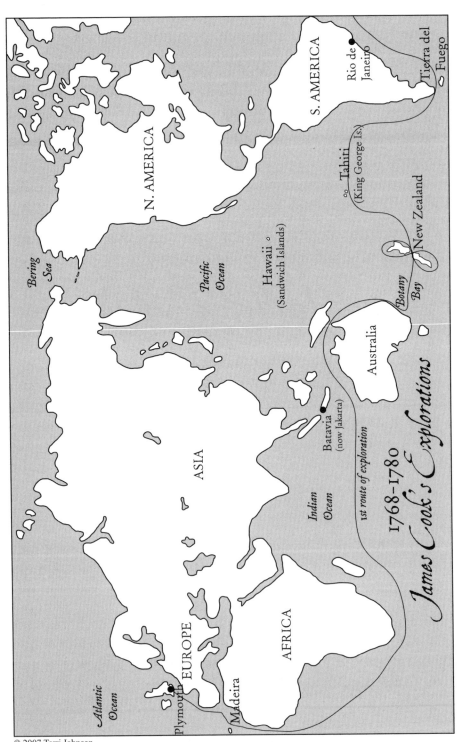

James Cook's Explorations

1768–1780

# III

# James Cook

## Explorer of the South Seas

*by Jocelyn James*

He crouched in the boat, hardly daring to breathe. His every breath seemed to pierce the silence of the night. Waiting quietly, he could hear the small ripples hitting the side of the boat, the wind rustling through the trees and the distant noises of the forest. Did he dare to look up? He strained and heard low Indian voices trailing away. He waited.

James straightened after what seemed like hours of hiding. He was tall and broad, so felt sore from the confinement. He dropped the line over the side again and continued to make his soundings. The work had become more dangerous now – he had almost been discovered this time. Shifting the crude piece of paper, he managed to gain a little more light and wrote down his calculations. He knew that this would be the last night of mapping this unpredictable river.

It was with great pleasure that James Cook, master's mate, went to see General Wolfe the next day. In his hands was the charting of the

St Lawrence River, and with it, the means to navigate a safe passage for the English ships to the city of Quebec. This alone would not win the war with the French for the wilds of Canada, but it would certainly give the English the foothold they needed. James had known how dangerous and important this work would be, which is why most of it had been done after dark. So night after night, Cook had gone in a small boat, sometimes alone and sometimes with other men. He checked the depth of the water, noted the dangerous shoals, and charted the narrowing shoreline. His charts were so accurate that, over time, not one of the 200 English ships that sailed down the river to a bank opposite Quebec was endangered. After Quebec fell, England began to win the war.

In 1762, as the Seven Year's War was drawing to a close, James found himself restless. What was to be his commission? He hungered for advancement, to show how capable he was if given the chance. He continued to do chart work and to be master's mate aboard Lord Colville's ship. Though Colville treated him well, it seemed he would not be given another position or an offer of advancement. James brooded over the letter he was writing. He would not write all of his thoughts in his letter to Elizabeth, since he knew she could not fully understand his restlessness. Besides, it was not something to write when courting a lady.

He was interrupted by a visitor, Captain Pallister. Hugh Pallister was tall and slender, with a noble bearing. His brown eyes glanced down to take in Cook's correspondence.

"Sir, I did not see you there," remarked James.

"I won't interrupt you for long, Cook – I can see you are busy. Have you given any thought to what you will do now?"

"I have been wondering if I will be discharged after the war and have to go back to hauling coal."

"Your work has been invaluable. Not only did you help us gain access to Quebec, but the more thorough charting of the river afterwards bears great testimony to your skill," said Pallister. "I'm sure there will be another commission for you."

"Thank you, sir," James said with some relief. "I have always benefited from your attention. Indeed, I would not have advanced this far in the Service without it."

"Nonsense!" Hugh replied. "Any recommendation I have made for your advancement was based on merit. You may not have been born to a noble family, James, but you were born to the sea."

Ironically, James Cook had been born to a farming family in the north of England. His father, James senior, may have expected his son to take over the farm from him one day, but he realized early that his son had no interest in it. Even after he was apprenticed to a storekeeper, James was not happy. He would often daydream, gazing out of the window at the seaport near by. This shop was close enough to the sea that James could feel the breezes, hear the waves and the noise of the men at anchor. What began as a daydream, grew to a passion that burned within him. He knew that no other course would satisfy. He must find his way to sea.

When James finally gathered his courage and went to the collier's yard, he was a lad of 17. Almost fully grown, strong and fit from hauling boxes at the store, he cut an imposing figure. John Walker, the owner of the shipyard, saw immediately that this young man had the drive and commitment to be a seaman, even though he was coming to the profession very late.

While James did not find the fulfillment he craved in those years, he did learn everything he needed to know on board a ship. He battled storms off the coast of England, fought harsh waves in the Baltic Sea, and coped with the incessant fog and rain as any seaman must. He taught himself astronomy so he could navigate a ship by the stars. He learned mathematics and read all he could about exploration. His thirst for the sea continued to grow along with his knowledge and skill.

He was about to be given the command of his own vessel, when he told Walker that he was joining the Navy. Cook knew that his employer would question his sense of duty, but James knew where that duty lay. England was on the brink of war with France. If he did not join now, he could easily be pressed into service, anyway. In this way, he could choose both his captain and his ship.

So Cook left his work as a collier, hauling coal in little ships up and down the coast of England, and embarked upon his life in the Navy. From the beginning, Captain Pallister saw that Cook was an accomplished and ambitious man. They spent almost two years together as captain and master. Mutual friendship, admiration and respect grew between them that lasted throughout their lives. Whenever their paths crossed, Sir Hugh Pallister found another way to advance James Cook's career.

After the English won the war against France, James remained in Canada for another five years. While Hugh Pallister certainly helped him, James' work spoke for itself. Cook was given the responsibility of charting the Newfoundland area. He did this work over the summer months and returned to England in the winter to draw up the maps. On his trip to England in 1762, James married Elizabeth Batts.

It is hard to know what she thought when, after a few months of married life, and already pregnant, she had to say goodbye to her husband for most of the following year. In fact, it became the pattern of Elizabeth's life as James continued in the Navy.

A man sat on a stone bench in the middle of Hyde Park. He was solid and flushed in the cheeks from his indulgent lifestyle. Better known for his midnight snack than his career, Lord Sandwich waited impatiently. A few minutes later, a much younger man, slender and well dressed, sat down beside him.

"Sorry to be late, my Lord," Joseph Banks said.

"Yes, yes," Lord Sandwich said brusquely. "What have you to report?"

"I have just come from a meeting at the Royal Society and a man by the name of James Cook is now being considered," he said.

Alexander Dalrymple, a famous geographer, had been the Society's choice to lead an expedition into the Pacific. The mission was to observe the transit of Venus across the sun. Edmond Hally had predicted that this would occur in 1769, and the Royal Society and Royal Observatory wanted it witnessed from different points of the globe. Dalrymple also believed there was an immense southern continent waiting to be found and was eager to be the one to find it.

"Yes, Dalrymple's chances are gone now. The fool should have realized that the Admiralty would never give command of a Navy ship to a civilian!" barked Sandwich. "Tell me more about this Cook fellow."

"He didn't come up through the normal Academy ranks. He isn't even the son of a nobleman. He's served the Navy well and is something of a scientist himself. Apparently, he wrote a paper on a solar eclipse he witnessed when he was in Newfoundland last year. He is almost forty, married, with 3 children," Banks continued.

"Seems unusual to give such an honorable post to a man who hasn't even made captain," Lord Sandwich remarked. "Who are his sponsors? That will tell us what we need to know."

"I believe Governor Pallister and Lord Colville have given him commendations," Banks replied. For someone so young, Joseph Banks was extremely well connected. "I think it is a good choice. If you will sponsor me to have the role as a naturalist, I believe I could work with someone in his position."

"I think that can be arranged," Lord Sandwich mused. "With the French and Spanish opposition to any exploration work done by the English, perhaps a less-titled sea captain is prudent."

Not long after this, in May 1768, James Cook was commissioned as a lieutenant and given command of the *HMS Endeavour Bark*. Though usually a reserved man, James showed his enthusiasm for the promotion by throwing himself into preparations for the voyage. The ship was being refitted at Deptford, and James made sure he was there to oversee the work.

The weeks dragged by and Elizabeth neared the end of her fourth pregnancy. The date set for departure made it clear that James would be gone again before she gave birth. The summer was reaching its fullness and the prolonged heat made conditions seem oppressive to James on land. With the exception of leaving Elizabeth, he was happy to be escaping to the freshness of the sea.

Cook's mind turned from his family to the adventure that was beginning. He put the little writing desk Elizabeth had given him into the great cabin. This small wooden box, filled with his paper and inks, was a wonderful present. After they sailed down the Thames, James heard a loud thump. It reminded him of an incident that had occurred a month earlier when he was showing Joseph Banks the finished vessel.

"Mr. Banks, what seems to be the problem?" Cook had asked.

"Captain, you expect me to have this…this tiny storeroom as my quarters?" Banks had replied tersely.

All the finery of London could not buy Mr. Banks a palace on a ship, Cook had thought to himself. He replied in a more polite manner. "Mr. Banks, we must all make do on a long trip such as this. Your cabin is almost as large as mine." James had stood up in Banks's cabin and bumped his head as he had done so.

"Where am I to put all the samples I collect? Surely we could have some space in the Great cabin for our scientific work?" Banks had asked.

"As long as you realize that my work is done there, too, Mr. Banks. The maps and charts will need to have room, but I believe this request can be accommodated."

Each man had sized up the other. Though they were from vastly different worlds, both were dedicated to their work. They would have to accommodate each other if they were to survive the voyage ahead.

This was tested some months later when the ship took on provisions in Madeira. Among the supplies were almost 4000 pounds of onions as well as cabbages and other vegetables.

"Captain," said Joseph Banks as he stood at the door of the Great Cabin.

"Yes, Mr. Banks," said James, as he looked up from his calculations. He was trying to position the ship's longitude. This was an exacting science and usually took several hours.

"Am I truly to believe this last order? You expect me to eat a... a...whole plate of onions?" What is the meaning of this?" cried Banks, exasperated.

Cook looked at the twenty-five year old man. He had led a very luxuriant and sheltered life in England. This trip was a new education for him.

"Mr. Banks, I presume you have not done any reading on ways

to combat scurvy?" Looking at the bewildered face, it was a somewhat rhetorical question. "Mr. Banks, I will humor your questioning my order this time, since you are not a man of the sea. I have seen the effects of this disease upon men as I traveled to and from Canada. I have read of many devastating cases on long sea voyages. From what I have read, fresh produce is required. As a man's diet becomes weak, so too does his constitution. Whenever we have fresh supplies, each man will eat the ration apportioned to him — from the captain down. Is that clear, Mr. Banks?" he said firmly.

In disgust, Joseph gave in. Though he, among others, did not relish the prospect of the onions, the sauerkraut, nor any of the other anti-scurvy measures, they were eaten. An understanding developed between the captain and the crew. While vexing at times, they knew their captain was working in their best interests.

After several more months of sailing, the *Endeavour* reached King George's Island, known to the locals as Tahiti. The white and golden beaches, the clear blue waters, the smell of ripening tropical fruits, the dazzling sunlight, the warmth of the air all assailed the senses of the men. Though they had heard of the place before their departure, nothing had prepared them for the reality. It was a paradise!

Cook assembled all the men on deck and spoke to them solemnly. "Men, we have reached our destination. Remember, we are the strangers here. We want to ensure good relations with these people and for them to know that we respect them and wish to work with them. You are to do no bartering of your own. Any trades are to be done by me, Mr. Gore, or any other officers approved by me." He knew there was little more he could say. When he was at sea, he commanded the vessel and the men were kept in order by their daily routines. He read the services from the prayer book on Sundays and tried to instill a moral discipline in the

James Cook

men. However, when on shore, he knew that they would find their own leisure. He hoped none of their conduct would lead to bad relations with the natives.

The next six months were an adjustment for both sides. The Tahitians were friendly and had a thriving culture of their own. Everything they used they made by hand, often from wood, but also using thick leaves, vines, feathers and shells. Having access to metal was new to them, and they bartered as much as they could for even one small nail. Bartering, of course, was only one way to gain access to the goods of value. Cook and the crew soon found that the Tahitians had a very different view about personal property.

"It's not here!" he cried. "It was here yesterday and I'm sure I left it right in this spot." Mr. Green was becoming very agitated now. What should he do? He checked again and realized there was no other course of action; he must report the theft to the Captain.

Moments later, James Cook came into the tent. They had spent months constructing a fort on one side of the island, ready to observe the transit of Venus. Now, the actual event was only a few days away.

"Mr. Green, you asked to see me?"

"Yes, most urgently, for I cannot find the quadrant I left here yesterday. It's missing or has been taken," Green said with a broken voice.

"Mr. Green, which is it to be? Have you mislaid it, or has it been stolen?" Cook was trying not to sound alarmed. Green, who had been appointed by the Royal Observatory to watch the transit, would not manage without this valuable instrument. How could they accurately record the progression of Venus across the face of the sun?

"I believe it has been stolen, sir," Green ventured at last. "There is no other explanation for its whereabouts."

"Or lack thereof," said Cook sternly. "The Tahitians must have taken it. Our men know its purpose and would hardly squander it for any other. I'm afraid it will call for drastic measures – we have no time to waste."

Cook ordered to have one of the more powerful Tahitians chiefs brought to him. He would be held captive until the quadrant was recovered. In under a day, the Tahitians responded to the demands for its return. It came back, piece by piece. Green was in despair because he would have to reconstruct the device quickly. Through hard work and effort, it was done in time. The transit was observed without further hinderance, although the reliability of Green's recordings was later disputed.

Soon after the transit, the Englishmen departed the beautiful setting and James turned to the other orders given to him by the Admiralty. They had been secret until he completed the mission in Tahiti. He opened them now, in the great cabin with Mr. Gore.

"It says we are to go to New Zeeland, chart the island, and then look for the great southern continent and claim it for England," said Cook.

"If there is one to be found," said Mr. Gore, his disbelief evident in his tone.

"I see you take my view of things. The Dutch have been in these waters more than any one else and have found no such continent. Perhaps New Zeeland and New Holland are part of some greater land mass, but a great southern continent to rival those in the North?"

Cook cut himself off, "On to New Zeeland, Mr. Gore."

Mr. Gore knew he was dismissed. He left Cook rearranging Banks' botanical samples so he could spread out his charts on the table.

After several months of sailing, a young boy in the rigging called,

"Land, ho!" All were grateful that New Zeeland was where the Dutch had said it would be. Cook came onto the main deck and watched as they neared shore. Mr. Banks was on deck too, with most of his party. They were keen to be on land again. Not only was it better than the confinement of the ship, but there was another new world for them to explore.

When they put in to shore, they saw that the indigenous population closely resembled the Tahitians. Was it possible that they were in some way related? Banks had insisted that, along with taking various cultural artifacts from Tahiti, they also bring with them a male Tahitian to show the Royal Society. This man, Tupia, tried to converse with the natives in New Zealand and found they had a similar tongue. The culture, however, was vastly different. James looked at these men before him. Their faces were thickly tattooed on one side in a mural pattern, and they used bone and metal for decorations and weaponry. Their fine cloaks of feather and fur and their proud stance showed that they were a race of warriors. Even their war ships were strong, imposing, and expertly carved from a rich wood, with ghoulish figures adorning the sides. Cook rightly sensed that they must be cautious with these people. Guns were carried in defense whenever they were on shore seeking provisions. Their defensiveness was warranted, for this was the fearsome Maori of New Zealand. On later trips to the area, the English would discover that some were cannibals.

Cook did not linger and soon they were on board ship again. Joseph Banks stormed up to him after the ship was in deeper waters.

"What is the meaning of this?" he cried.

"Mr. Banks, I made it clear that our stay would be of short duration. My instructions are to chart the coast of New Zeeland, and I cannot do that from shore," Cook replied.

"My instructions are to gather as many samples and species of worth for the Royal Society. I can hardly do that on board ship!" Joseph retorted.

"Quite so, Mr. Banks. As you are on a ship provided by His Majesty's Navy, you must defer to my orders." Cook said firmly.

"Haven't I paid more than any one else to be a part of this voyage? " Banks fumed.

"We are most grateful, Mr. Banks, and I will accommodate you whenever I can."

Banks did not stay to converse any longer. Loud banging noises were heard below deck.

The charting of New Zealand, as Cook called it, took six months, and much to Banks' chagrin, most of that time was spent at sea. The wonderful islands, with their cool temperatures, lush green hills, and snow capped peaks remained out of Banks' reach. In a way, he did not mind. He did not share Cook's love of the Maori. He preferred the fun-loving and relaxed Tahitians to this sterner, more imposing race. He also did not share Cook's thrill in finding that there were two islands instead of one, nor his enthusiasm for naming various points and rivers. He longed to go ashore again.

The *Endeavour* departed New Zealand courtesy of a violent storm. Waves engulfed the ship, making it seem like a dinghy in a tempest. The winds howled and ripped their way across the decks. Even in the cabin, the motion was so violent that no rest could be had. Banks stayed below, barely hearing the Captain shout orders to his men to combat the storm.

When it abated after several days, they realized they had been blown off-course. It seemed of little matter, for land was sighted in the distance. As they drew closer, they saw it was not as fertile as the coast they had left behind in New Zealand, though it still looked quite good.

Though all were eager to land, they sailed on. Cook was looking through his glass as they continued up the coast. The ship needed a safe place to put in for repairs, as well as an area that was well provisioned. Banks did not understand this and exhibited his impatience to be on land again.

"Ah, Mr. Banks," said Cook. "I think I have found the place. You can tell your entourage that we will be landing soon and there will be plenty of time for them to gather their specimens."

"Sir, I was just coming to discuss the matter with you." He paused, and then said, "I am glad of it. Thank you,"

The area proved to be filled with a wide variety of flora and fauna hitherto unknown to the botanical community. After several suggestions, Cook named the place Botany Bay. One of the lovely native flowers was later named a "Banksia" in honor of the naturalist. Banks and his team remained busy, cataloguing their specimens and making sketches of all they could.

Cook continued in his determined and detailed way. Another six months was spent charting the coast of this new land. Cook was as excited as Banks, but for another reason. He poured over maps in the great cabin and continued to work on his own. Suddenly, there was a knock at the door. James looked up and motioned for Mr. Gore, his first lieutenant, to enter.

"Sir, you are working late," Mr. Gore said, leaving the reproof unfinished. He knew this man was extremely dedicated.

James, still in a trance, slowly turned his head. "Mr. Gore, I am quite running out of names. You must help me," he said, excitedly. Mr. Gore had not seen him like this. In the privacy of his own space, Cook could show the enthusiasm he felt. He had studied all the maps of the Pacific, all the writings of the Dutch, and knew that they had stumbled upon something unknown before now. Perhaps it was part of New

Holland, an eastern coast but no one had ever charted it before. This was his opportunity to put his mark on the world map.

"Here, this one! What should we name it?" he said earnestly.

Mr. Gore gazed at him and then at the scroll unfurled on the desk. Before he had a chance to answer, Cook spoke again, in a less animated fashion. "You are quite right, it is late. Anyway, think on it, Gore, and let me know tomorrow."

The next day, however, naming was the last thing on their minds. As they proceeded along the vast coast, Cook wanted to stay close to the shoreline so that he could chart as much of it as possible. This was starting to become dangerous as the water kept changing depths. Sometimes it was 20 fathoms deep, and a short distance later it had dropped to 8. Though Cook was at a loss to explain this situation, it required his diligence and careful attention. There was no time for idle chat.

That night, soon after Cook had gone to bed, a horrible screeching was heard down one whole side of the ship. It creaked and groaned and grew louder with each passing moment. Something was horribly wrong. Still in his nightcap and night shirt, he bounded back up onto the deck. The captain in him came to the fore immediately as he barked out the necessary orders to his crew. The commotion woke Banks and his party as well. Though they came topside to see what the matter was, there was little they could do. They watched, dumbfounded, as the crew tried to plug the gash in the hull. Men could be seen in the moonlight, straining, pushing, pulling, pumping, to get the excess water off the ship. The threat of shipwreck was real, and each man worked with an energy borne of desperation, in a form of measured frenzy for the rest of the night.

Mr. Gore came over to the captain and said, "There's a midshipman here who claims to know how to stop the leak."

Cook was still ordering supplies and cannons to be taken out of the ship to lighten her load. He was half distracted as Gore continued.

"He says he's seen it done on clipper ships in the American colonies. It's called fothering, sir. If we tar and oil the spare sail and put it around the hull of the ship, the water will draw the sail onto the ship and plug the hole."

"By all means, then, go ahead. If we can pump all the water out and make the high tide, we may just get out of this one," Cook said resolutely. He wiped his tired, furrowed brow. It would take a miracle. They were stuck half way around the globe, in previously unchartered waters, with no idea how far away from any civilized port they might be. If they survived, he would strongly recommend that no ship explore by itself again.

The *Endeavour* was able to continue its voyage at high tide two days later. They found a way to shore near the mouth of a river and beached the ship. When Cook saw the hole in the ship, he was amazed. A huge piece of brightly colored coral was stuck fast to the hull. They had sailed through what is now known as the Great Barrier Reef. Sailors still marvel that Cook and his crew were not shipwrecked, but managed to navigate through the dangerous reefs of coral back out to the open sea.

The beaching of the *Endeavour* meant weeks of time spent ashore working on repairs. For Banks and his party, it meant weeks for exploring. Here Banks discovered a strange animal with the face of a hare, fur that was the color of a mouse, small arms at the front and large, strong hind legs. It had a long tail and hopped around from place to place. Both Banks and Cook had trouble describing this animal in their journals but learned that the native Aborigines called it a "kanguru" and so, it became a "kangaroo" to the Englishmen.

One day, after a fruitful time collecting samples, Banks came toward the ship. He saw the captain working at his small desk near the ship and approached. James looked up from his papers.

"Mr. Banks, I am indebted to you for bringing your books with you. I think de Torres found a strait of water between New Guinea and New Holland. I am sure we have been sailing up the eastern coast of "New Holland" for months. If this is correct, once we are out in open sea, we will meet up with this strait quite soon. Once repairs are completed, I mean to take this route to Batavia."

"Good, good," Joseph said, distractedly. "Aah, Mr. Cook, I believe we have a problem. It seems the natives want the turtles we have been killing for food. I think they believe the turtles and the land belong to them."

"We have caught the turtles for ourselves. The men have been working hard to keep up fresh provisions. I'm afraid we don't have enough to spare. We'll just have to tell them that," James remarked matter of factly. As much as possible, he had tried to work with the natives of any new areas they came to, but sometimes it was difficult. The Aborigines did not share Cook's ethics of hard work and enterprise. Their communal culture had different methods and expectations. In frustration, Cook felt that force was the only "reason" they understood. With each successive voyage, that force would become more violent.

James was happy when they finally left the newly named *Endeavour* River and started on their homeward journey. He stopped briefly at Cape York, satisfied it was the northern most tip of this land mass, and claimed the whole eastern coast line for King George, naming it "New South Wales". It took them almost another year to reach their beloved England, as they had to stop in the East Indies for months of repair work before heading around Africa and back home. They had been gone for nearly three years. Unfortunately, they had lost one third of their men, including Tupia, to malaria in Batavia.

When they returned in 1771, James went first to the Admiralty and reported. Afterward, he came back home to his wife and family. There, he discovered the devastating news that one of his children had died during his absence. Elizabeth had managed on her own, bore the grief, and kept on with the household affairs. James could only comfort her now.

Not long after, James was received at court and had an audience with King George. Joseph Banks was the toast of London. He would, however, have to wait until the successful return of the next voyage to have a Tahitian native to parade around at all the social gatherings. All were delighted with the trip and there seemed to be talk of another journey. Dalrymple was still not convinced that Cook had disproved the claim of a great southern continent. He said that Cook hadn't looked hard enough for it. This accusation angered James, for he knew he had sailed through much of the South Pacific. How could there be a larger unknown land mass? The thought niggled, and King George, Sir Hugh Pallister, now Comptroller of the Navy, and Lord Sandwich led the charge for another expedition. Of course, there was no one else to whom they would turn but James Cook. He was given a promotion to Commander, and within a year of his return, set off into the Pacific again. This time, at Cook's insistence, two ships made the journey.

Elizabeth faced years on her own with her growing family, and again, she bid him farewell with a swollen belly.

*Hyde Park, London ~ December* 1781

A man stood in the middle of the park. The gentle breeze caught his dark, wavy hair. He started to pace a little. He was unaccustomed to delays such as this. After all, he was an eminent man in his field and high in London society. His attendant alerted him that his companion had arrived by carriage.

"My Lord..."

"Sorry to keep you waiting, Banks. Get in. I prefer to take a tour of the park today," the Lord of the Admiralty replied.

Sir Joseph Banks, now the President of the Royal Society, sat on the opposite side of the carriage. Before he could speak, the lord continued.

"Those impertinent American colonists! Looks as though that is one war we are going to lose. There seems to be no hope after Yorktown," he barked. "If we do lose those colonies, you know what will happen, I suppose?"

Joseph arched an eyebrow but did not speak. He knew not to interrupt Lord Sandwich when he was in such a mood. After all, he had risen very prominently in recent years because of the way he had kept abreast of issues of importance.

"Our jails and all those hulks in the harbor are full again. Parliament will have to deal with this problem," he remarked, insightfully. Banks still looked on, waiting for what he suspected would come next.

"Where else can we send them?"

Banks looked upon the elderly man across from him in the carriage. "I think I have mentioned to you often how I loved Botany Bay above all other places I visited. I think even Captain James Cook would have agreed with me," he added.

"Ah, Cook. What a waste of a fine man! Cut down by those Hawaiian natives in the prime of his life!" Lord Sandwich replied.

Banks again did not reply, but waited for him to continue.

"Not sure I like the place of his death to be named after me.

Sandwich Islands! You know he's named far too many things after me. I've gone back through some of his maps and changed some so Cook's name is in there a bit more."

Lord Sandwich was helping to prepare Cook's last journals for publication.

"That's very benevolent of you, sir," Joseph replied.

"Well, that's by and by. You think Cook would have agreed with you? I always thought New Zealand was his favorite place. He described it in such glowing terms every time he went. Almost seemed like a little slice of a lush, English countryside was deposited on the other side of the globe."

"Yes, sir, he did love New Zealand above all others. I do believe that, because he loved it so much, he wouldn't want to see it touched or despoiled by our riff-raff. Actually, didn't you tell me about his last journals? He wanted us to stay away from the Pacific. He thought we had already tarnished these simple, child-like societies. Didn't you tell me that recently?"

Lord Sandwich nodded and Banks continued. "New South Wales, therefore, is one of the best choices. The natives are far less hostile than those Maori. It is fertile enough, and the expanse of the shoreline showed us that there is room to accommodate a settlement. Yes, I think Cook would heartily endorse my comments."

"Fine man, that Cook." Lord Sandwich remarked. "Never went with him on that second voyage – perhaps you should have."

Banks smarted a little at this rebuke. He had planned to go on the second voyage to find the southern continent but would not go on an inferior vessel. The ship could not accommodate all of his specifications for extra rooms, so he had withdrawn from the party.

"I think his first and third voyages were probably more

significant," he replied, trying to deflect the comment. "The second voyage was more about what he didn't find than what he actually did." Banks immediately regretted his hasty comment.

"Nonsense! To me, that second voyage was his greatest triumph! To sail for three whole years, lose only one man and none to scurvy? To sail to the depths of the earth, battle those bracing, icy winds and search doggedly for a continent that everyone assumed must be there? What persistence and what fortitude! To put all those astronomers in their place too! Who would have thought that a timepiece would solve the longitude problem? What a fantastic trial was made of it then. No, I think you missed out, Banks. Certainly would have been better to be on that one than with him at the end. Who knows, maybe you would have been killed too!" Lord Sandwich chuckled, clearly enjoying himself.

"Yes, sir," Banks said grudgingly, not sharing his humor. "Well, anyway, I will agree with you on his greatness. We may not always have seen eye to eye, but I believe we had a good friendship. We certainly lost a very fine man."

"Yes," Lord Sandwich replied solemnly and then moved on. "So, Botany Bay? You will have to carry the day on this one, Banks. I am going to retire in a few months and the wheels move very slowly on these things."

"I'm sorry to hear that, my Lord," Banks replied. "It would be my pleasure to tell the parliamentary committee itself, if need be."

*Epilogue*

Captain James Cook was killed at Kealakekua Bay in 1779. The Hawaiians believed Cook to be one of their gods, Lono, and welcomed his "return" to their islands. When Cook's ships were damaged not far from Hawaii and had to limp back to the bay, suspicions were aroused. When a man in Cook's charge died, they realized that this figure before them, who had so readily accepted their gifts and worship as a god was actually a mere man, with all of the frailties. In fact, it was while he was trying to sort out a dispute with the natives, that one stabbed him in the back. James Cook, who had done more to alter the map of the world peacefully than any other man[1], died a violent death.

Sir Joseph Banks gave a report to parliament in 1785 in such glowing terms that the decision was made to establish a colony in New South Wales. The first fleet landed in Botany Bay in 1788. Settlers came from England to New Zealand in the early 1800s, and a formal colony was founded in 1839. Wars with the Maori stained the years that followed.

Elizabeth Cook had six children in all, and lost two in their infancy. She lost another two in tragic circumstances. She survived all of her children and lived until she was 93. There were no grandchildren. Lord Sandwich provided for her financially and she gained income from the continued sales of her husband's journals. Hers was a private world and her James was also to remain private. She burnt all of his letters to her before she died.

1    pg 74 Bryce, G., *The Sketchbook of the HMS Endeavour* Sydney, Collins, 1983

*About the Author:*

Jocelyn James lives not far from Botany Bay in Canberra, Australia. Before children, Jocelyn taught English, History, and Art at High School level and now, she is teaching her 4 boys at home - with all its challenges and joys. Her favorite past times are reading, collecting books, drawing, writing and making cards. Jocelyn's biography of Constantine was published in *What Really Happened in Ancient Times*. She also writes periodically for two Australian homeschooling magazines, *A Living Education* and *Education Choices*. See her blog: www.homeschoolblogger.com/JocelynJames for more details.

*I lovingly dedicate Rachel Revere: the Ride of Her Life to Mrs. Patricia Johnson my sixth grade teacher at Cumberland Elementary School. Mrs. Johnson introduced me to Roget's Thesaurus and we have been dear friends ever since. The feedback she wrote on my first report encouraged me to keep writing. She called me a "delightful storyteller" and it stuck! Thank you, Mrs. Johnson, for awaking hidden talents and inspiring a dream within me.*

# Rachel Walker Revere

## The Ride of Her Life

### 1745 - 1813

by Linda Ann Crosby

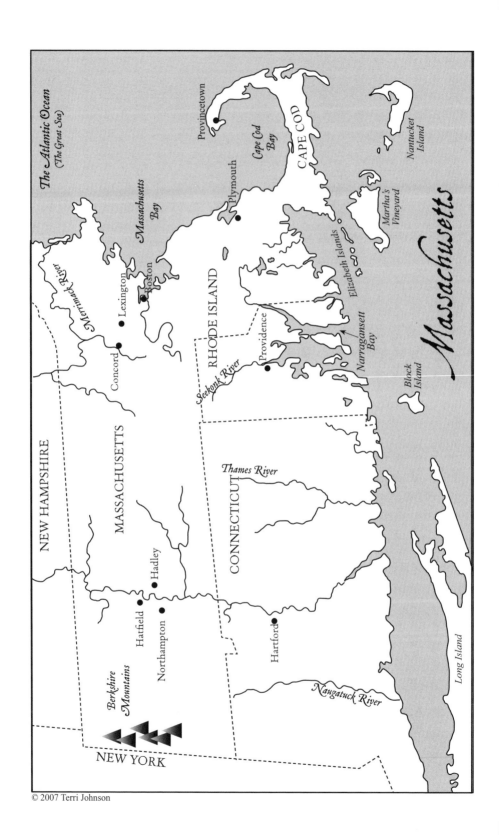

The Atlantic Ocean
(The Great Sea)

Provincetown

Cape Cod Bay

CAPE COD

Nantucket Island

Martha's Vineyard

Massachusetts Bay

Plymouth

Merrimack River

Lexington

Boston

Elizabeth Islands

Concord

RHODE ISLAND

Providence

Narragansett Bay

Seekonk River

Black Island

Massachusetts

NEW HAMPSHIRE

MASSACHUSETTS

Thames River

CONNECTICUT

Hadley

Hatfield

Northampton

Hartford

Berkshire Mountains

Naugatuck River

Long Island

NEW YORK

# IV

# Rachel Walker Revere

## The Ride of Her Life

*by Linda Ann Crosby*

*Boston, Province of Massachusetts, New England ~ Late Summer 1765 ~*

*M*other, please do not pull my laces as you did yester eve. Barely could I breathe for my stays were so tight," lamented Rachel as she held onto the bedpost.

"Nonsense!" said her mother impatiently. "You know how important it is that you look presentable at all times. One never knows when the Lord might put a handsome man in your path."

Rachel looked heavenward as if questioning God on the same topic. *Why am I still a maid at the age of twenty?* she wondered. Throughout her life she had been told she was beautiful, with her long, straight nose, high forehead and curly brown hair. Her eyes, her father once observed, "are as large and brown as a cow's eyes." This was meant to be a compliment but being compared to a farm animal did not sit well with Rachel. It was indeed a mystery why Rachel Walker was yet unwed, as she was not unbecoming and her neighborliness drew people to her.

Most women Rachel's age were married and having their second and third children by the age of twenty. But Rachel was biding her time between helping her mother tend their home, and assisting her two great aunties who lived in a handsome house once owned by her great-grandfather on Clark's Wharf.

"I am only going to see the Aunts today and no men are ever in that house," Rachel commented. It was true. Aside from Father, the last man to enter that home had been Rachel's one and only suitor. "That man is so frail looking," Rachel had told her father, "I am sure I could swing him around over my head. Really, Father! He is certainly not God's idea of a husband for me." The memory caused Rachel to smile. Her father had not done any matchmaking since then, for now he was preoccupied with the political happenings in Boston.

The presence of British troops was almost non-existent in town. In January, the English Parliament had enacted the Stamp Act in the colonies. The monies collected were supposed to pay the costs for British soldiers stationed in the western frontier. It was odd to Rachel that the people of New England were required to pay a tax to issue and buy the business papers that had for years been free. Ship's papers, marriage licenses, legal documents, newspapers, even playing cards were taxed. The French and Indian War had ended two years ago. Many colonists wondered why troops were still needed near the Appalachian Mountains.

A new society, called the Sons of Liberty, formed to protest England's attempts at governing New England without any input from the colonies. 'Taxation without representation' was the new phrase being passed along the streets of Boston. Samuel Adams was the founder of this new society. Their purpose was to raise the awareness of the colonists that their liberties were being taken away by England.

The Distributor of Stamps for Massachusetts was Andrew Oliver.

As the king's representative, he was the target of the first act of the Sons of Liberty. A scarecrow of sorts was made in the image of Mr. Oliver and was hung in a large elm tree. The episode lasted all day, gathering a crowd that intimidated the officers who were ordered to remove the display. A commotion at dusk drew Rachel out of doors into the warm evening air to see a huge multitude taking down the exhibit. Many politicians, tradesmen and artisans belonging to the Sons of Liberty led the crowd. Among them Rachel recognized Samuel Adams, Paul Revere and John Hancock. Rachel knew these men as upstanding leaders in society. They passed through the streets chanting, "Liberty, Property, and No Stamps."

Samuel Adams, a man of forty-three years, conducted business in town. He was a newly elected member of the Massachusetts legislature. Samuel was married to a woman named Elizabeth and had two children.

Paul Revere was a silversmith, engraver and dentist who lived in a house owned by Dr. Clark, right next door to Rachel's Aunts' home on the wharf. He was not a tall man but his shoulders were as broad as a bull's. At the age of thirty-one, Mr. Revere was married and had several children, maybe four, that Rachel had seen playing in the garden behind their home.

John Hancock, at twenty-eight years, was the most eligible bachelor in Boston. He was a tall, thin, flashy man, who wore lavender suits of silk and satin. His rags to riches upbringing was a favorite story for wagging chins. John was an orphan, adopted by a rich uncle who had a shipping empire. He worked beside his uncle in the family business. When Rachel was fifteen John had been the talk of the town, for he was sent on a business mission to England and witnessed the crowning of George III, the King of England. Sadly, only three years later, his uncle passed away. At that time John inherited the largest fortune in New

England.

Rachel took pride in being a British subject and loved to hear of their new young king. George III became king at the age of twenty-two after the death of his grandfather. Stories drifted across the waters to the colonies that George III had chosen a princess from Germany to be his wife. Her name was Princess Charlotte of Mecklenburg and she was a mere sixteen-years-old. The King had arranged the whole wedding, including Charlotte's dress, tiara and eleven attendants. It sounded so romantic to loveless Rachel, and at the same time made her feel like an old maid at twenty.

Rachel didn't understand why so many in Boston were in an uproar about a few taxes Parliament had imposed. Hopefully all the hubbub would die down and life in New England would continue as it had.

*~ Early Spring 1770 ~*

With dismal skies outside, Rachel lit an oil lamp next to her dressing table in order to see her reflection in the small oval mirror. She was brushing out her mass of curls and relishing the view from the second story of her great Aunts' home on Clark's Wharf. Rachel truly loved watching the endless activities of the bustling port populated by 16,000 people. Even at the age of twenty-five, she marveled at how childlike she was, fascinated by the colorful sights, clamoring sounds and fishy smells of the wharf.

From this very window, in February, Rachel watched as Mr. Revere, his wife Sara, the elder Mrs. Revere and their now six children, move out of the cozy house next door. Rachel noticed that Mrs. Revere was indeed about to have their seventh child, and they certainly needed more elbow room. They purchased a one-hundred-year-old frame home for their growing family on North Square. It wasn't more than three blocks away, but she would miss seeing the children playing and Mrs. Revere hanging her dish towels on the gooseberry bushes in the yard.

North Square was an unusual name for the triangular shaped clearing that housed one of the town pumps, a market and a guardhouse in the center of Boston. It was a well-to-do and respectable part of town, consisting of neatly kept small homes, most adjoining their neighbors. There were picket fences bordering trimmed yards, shop signs advertising all sorts of wares and services as well as the 'Old North Meeting' which was the 'church of the Mathers.' Four generations of Mather ministers had graced the pulpit, and it was the worship hall of choice for many Puritan families in Boston.

Snow had been heavily falling all day and Rachel stayed near the large, brick fireplace in her aunt's kitchen working on her third cross-stitch sampler. Most girls barely tied the final knot on their first sampler before they were married. Rachel's skill with a needle and thread had certainly improved since her initial sampler, and she took pleasure in turning the colorful threads into delicate letters, numbers and a flowered border. In between stitches, Rachel's time was spent tending the reflector oven by turning the crank until the roast duck was cooked all around. She eventually put the duck in the brazier to keep it hot until dinnertime.

Rachel, her father and mother, and the two aunts ate dinner late that evening and lingered at the large, roughly hewn wooden table discussing the changes in and around Boston. At 9:00 p.m. the church bells began ringing an alarm from the surrounding churches. Rachel's father instructed them to stay in the house while he hastily threw on his coat followed by his heavy black great coat. As he departed, Rachel heard gunfire, several shots being fired in a burst. The women huddled together near the fireplace, praying that their husband, nephew and father would return unharmed.

At 10:15 p.m. Rachel's father burst through the door with dismay written on his face. "There was a mob scene in front of the Customs House on King Street," he got out between breaths. "They began harassing the soldier on guard, throwing snowballs, stones, and pieces of wood." As he peeled off layers of outerwear, he continued. "He called for help and nine fully armed sentry came scurrying to his aid. The people continued to throw snowballs and rocks. In the commotion 'Fire!' was heard and the soldiers began shooting at the townspeople." In shock, all four women drew their hands to their faces. "Blood covered the snow. Four men fell dead on the spot, one was a colored man, and five more were hurt."

"Were the soldiers arrested?" Rachel asked.

"Not yet, but from the cries of the townspeople, justice will prevail," her father reassured her.

The following week the soldiers were indeed kept in jail awaiting trial. Rachel saw firsthand the entire scene in a print from a copper engraving by Paul Revere. It showed the red-coated soldiers lined up and firing their weapons into the crowd. Captain Preston was depicted raising his sword as if to yell, "Fire!" Rachel also noticed that all of the men on the ground were white skinned. From her father's report, she knew that one of the men was a dark skinned man. It was apparent that Mr. Revere's engraving was not entirely truthful and had been designed to make the most of the massacre. The shooting was bad enough and Rachel did not see the need to capitalize on it. However, the Sons of Liberty desired to raise the awareness of the colonists. England would not let them govern themselves and the regulars would not back down even though there were only 600 redcoats stationed in and around Boston.

~ *Summer* 1773 ~

"Why don't you pick some herbs from the kitchen garden and take them around to the Revere home, Rachel," her mother suggested. "I've heard their baby is not well, and with the passing of their mother, the workload on that grandmother must be immense."

Rachel adored children and she missed seeing the Revere family playing together and singing songs in their backyard when they had been neighbors. She picked a basket off the mantle and gathered some sprigs of thyme, comfrey, lady's mantle and bayberries. Rachel didn't think twice about walking over to their home in her undress. This was not a formal call, and more than likely, Mr. Revere would be at his shop down on the wharf. Her simple cotton day gown with the ruffled lace tucker at her neck would suffice. The wind from the sea caught her sable curls and tugged them free from beneath her mob cap as she walked briskly three blocks uptown.

As Rachel turned the corner off of Fish Street she bumped into someone, scattering her herbs to the ground. She excused her clumsiness and began picking up the stems. She then noticed the gentleman was also gathering her herbs. As they stood, she looked into the eyes of Paul Revere. Immediately she was conscious of her casual attire and took notice of her billowing curls, trying unsuccessfully to tuck them back in.

"Miss Walker, where are you headed in such haste?" he asked.

"Your house.... I heard that your baby ....mother said the herbs.... not expect to see you.... the shop and ..." Rachel stammered tongue-tied and flustered.

Paul found this comical and was restraining himself from a full smile. "I've just come from home, but why don't I escort you back there to make certain you don't bowl over any more good townsfolk."

95

Rachel went right to work setting the kitchen straight in the Revere home. Paul had aptly trained daughters that were carrying on in their mother's absence. Sensing their need to be commended and encouraged, Rachel lovingly offered both. Her next task was administering the herbs, which had been boiled into a tea, for baby Isanna. She would take a sip or two from the silver sucking bottle before turning her head in protest. Rachel's heart sank. After making sure the family was set for their evening meal, Rachel tramped home burying her thoughts in her own meal preparations.

Paul Revere, on the other hand, was consumed with the lovely Rachel Walker. The following day at his silversmith shop, instead of designing a tea set that had been ordered by a British officer, the memory of a dark-haired beauty kept interfering with his work. The fire in the forge crackled and hissed. His apprentices, along with his son Paul, hammered away at the silver pieces they were shaping. But Paul was oblivious to the noise. He could not get Rachel out of his mind. Conversation with her came easily after her initial embarrassment vanished, and she had a cheerful disposition. Having seven children to raise, along with his elderly mother in his home, Paul was indeed in search of a new wife. Would Rachel be willing to marry a man nine years her senior with a house full of children? Paul prayed it so. Thus distracted, he wrote a poem on the back of a bill for mending a spoon, using clues to parts of Rachel's name. It read:

> *Take three fourths of a Paine that makes Traitors confess* (Rac, or rack)
> *With three parts of a place which the Wicked don't Bless* (hell)
> *Joyne four sevenths of an Exercise which shop-keepers use* (walk)
> *And what Bad men do, when they good actions refuse* (er, or err)
> *These four added together with great care and Art*
> *Will point out the Fair One nearest my Heart.*

As Paul began making appearances at the Walker's home morning, afternoon and evening, his care and concern for Rachel became apparent. Her father lovingly chided Rachel one evening, "Mr. Revere doesn't appear to be the type of man that you could swing around over your head." Paul was indeed a man of solid stature for which Rachel was thankful. Rachel returned his affections and, to the delight of the entire Walker family, consented to become Mrs. Paul Revere. Although the Reveres were members of Boston's New Brick Church, the marriage vows were repeated in October under a cool, but cloudless sky, guided by Reverend Samuel Mather from the Old North Meeting.

The dream of being a wife and mother materialized for Rachel with two simple words, "I do." She was thrust into the care and keeping of an extremely busy household. Rachel was grateful for the assistance of Paul's eldest daughters, the guidance of her new stepmother, Deborah, and the loving and deepening relationship with her new husband.

Shortly after they were wed, sorrow filled the Revere home as they laid little Isanna in the ground next to her mother's grave. The death was heartbreaking for Rachel as the child had clung to her as if she were her birth mother.

Rachel admired Paul's dedication to being home each evening so he could sit around the dinner table with his family, and then spend the evening with 'his lambs' until they were all tucked into bed. This heartwarming time should have made Rachel's heart sing, yet it grew to be the most frustrating time of her day. For as soon as the last child was kissed good night, Paul would leave until the wee hours of the morning. She became quietly reserved as evening approached, lips tentatively pressed into a firm line, her gentle mannerisms brisk, even slightly harsh. What had been unknown to her before their wedding, Rachel soon discovered. Paul was an active member, not only of the Sons of Liberty, but also of the Masonic Lodge, as well as the Committee of Correspondence. His nighttime engagements were secret meetings for the cause of liberty.

During their brief courting and in the first weeks of marriage, Paul would drive Rachel out to the Blue Hills of Milton, over to Cambridge, to Roxbury and to Watertown with his sorrel mare. These were Rachel's first journeys outside of her port town. She relished the expansive fields of the countryside, the plethora of green hues in the trees so lacking in Boston, and the magenta and crimson wildflowers. One afternoon, while driving back from Cambridge, Rachel expressed her displeasure at his increasing nightly abscences. The previous evening had been particularly vexing as he had only come home at the first hint of dawn. She soon discovered that her husband was the first choice of the Committee of Correspondence for the hardest rides throughout the thirteen colonies. His role of informing each province's leaders was vital to the unity of the colonies.

"How will each province know what the British are about if I do not ride?" Paul asked Rachel as a response to her questioning his involvement. "I need to deliver the writings from the committees so the representatives can jointly resist British rule."

"I apologize for seeming disrespectful, Paul," Rachel answered as she moved closer to him on the carriage seat. "I'm concerned for your safety."

Wrapping his free arm around her, Paul said, "My dear, I'm known by the Brits as a silversmith and engraver. Both give me reason to travel, delivering to customers. The officers let me pass without as much as my name and calling."

Rachel's fears were put to rest, not only by his words, but also by the tenderness of his embrace. She was beginning to understand the depth of Paul's conviction for New England's freedom from the mother country.

*~ December 1773 ~*

Rachel helped thirteen-year-old Paul Jr. place the cumbersome pail of snow by the fireplace where it would melt, providing much needed water. Severe weather, with blasting snow storms and frostbitten wind, slapped Boston much like the British taxes. The restricting climate limited Paul's rides, for which Rachel was grateful. Unfortunately, the cold did not force Paul indoors. His missions in the night were steady.

"Where in this freezing town do you go so late at night?" Rachel's voice seemed small from where she was snuggled beneath quilts on their feather tick.

Paul grinned at the sight of his wife. "To the Green Dragon, my love, to meet with likeminded men who want freedom for their families too." The tavern was owned by St. Andrew's Masonic Lodge, where Paul was a member, and was a central meeting place for patriots from all levels of society. Of stately brick structure, the lodge was suitably named for an ornate, copper dragon hanging on a pole above the entry.

"What was the tavern called before the copper dragon turned green?" Rachel coyly teased from her warm nest.

Paul paused from readying himself for bed. His forefinger and thumb stroked his broad chin as he replied, "I have never considered the initial days of the copper dragon, Rachel." The twinkle in his eye gleamed at her, reflecting the candlelight from the nightstand. "I shall bring that question forward next meeting when Sam Adams asks if there are any pressing measures to discuss."

The camaraderie between husband and wife increased daily

that first winter, as did the frost on the window panes. Late into the night, in the privacy of their bedroom, Paul would share with Rachel the restrictions and unfair demands handed down to the colonies from Parliament. As she absorbed her husband's words and opinions, Rachel's own sense of independence from England was growing. She was relieved when many taxes were repealed, yet didn't comprehend why Paul insisted that the wee tax on tea was intolerable.

"Resisting our much loved tea is purely a matter of proving a point to England. Rachel, we do not need their governing and will not buy their tea, no matter how small the amount of taxation."

Sipping a cup of English tea was as precious to Rachel as a moment of solitude in her home, filled as it was with children. However, she would stand with Paul on his decisions and go without tea as soon as her stores were depleted. A few days following their discussion, there were only enough leaves for a final pot in the Revere household. Rachel readied the teapot and gathered everyone around the table. "Children, this is the last cup of tea you will get for a long time," she regretfully told them as she poured. Each one savored the warmth and goodness down to the final sip.

In mid-December, the *Dartmouth* pulled into Griffin's Wharf brimming with chests full of tea from the British East India Company. The colonists rallied together to guard the ship, not allowing it to be unloaded. They hoped to force its return to England, hulls still laden with tea. On the twentieth day in port, the cargo was scheduled to be seized by customs officers and sold at auction if the ship did not unload or depart. While the entire town counted down the days to seizure, two more tea ships arrived, amplifying the tension. The Sons of Liberty met to discuss the embargo and the looming deadline.

The skies were coal-black and the air frigid on the nineteenth eve from the Dartmouth's dropping anchor in the harbor. Rachel was tidying the last of dinner when Paul asked her the most ridiculous question.

"My dear, could you please fill a small pot with some soot for me? And do you have any grease left from the chicken you prepared?"

"Next thing I know you will request the feathers I plucked from the bird as well!" Rachel's eyes were wider than usual.

"You're right. What a grand idea," agreed Paul.

"If you are serious, Mr. Revere, you have some explaining to do... and promptly."

"Rachel," he came to her and held her hands in his. "I'll tell you anything you desire; only you will have to wait for my return. Now, the soot and grease, please."

Paul gathered his requests, a hatchet, and a red blanket before Rachel watched him slip out on his mysterious mission. She settled into the worn rocker by the smoldering fire to mend some garments. Rachel did not realize the depth of her fatigue, and soon she rested her curly head back against the chair, arms limp and eyes shut.

The SLAM of the door startled her, causing her to bolt from the chair. Fear gripped her heart as, in the dim light, she discerned the shape of an Indian in her kitchen. Rachel was speechless. The intruder was fiercely painted with war stripes and feathers sporadically dangled from his hair.

"No need to fear, my dear," came a calming, familiar voice. "It is I, Paul."

Never had Rachel been so relieved to see her husband, despite his ridiculous appearance. Paul removed the blanket wrapped around his shoulders and proceeded to retell the night's events as Rachel sat silently shaking her head.

"It was brilliant, my dear!" he said with a bubbling, child-like

Rachel Revere

excitement. "There were three groups of fifty men, all dressed as foolish as myself. We boarded the ships and whacked the tea chests open with hatchets and poured the tea into Boston Harbor. All 342 chests were emptied. You should have seen it, Rach. There were thousands of people watching silently from the surrounding wharves. It was a marvelous plan to show England that we will not stand for taxes!" Paul could barely contain himself as he paced the floor in a gleeful caper.

"Well, I never!" was all Rachel kept repeating, while shaking her head in disbelief. Her husband was acting like a ten-year-old boy who had just coated the neighbor's cat with wheel grease and escaped without being caught. She could only imagine 149 other grown men dressed like Indians in their kitchens telling the same tale to bewildered wives at this late hour.

Early the next morning there was a knock on the door by a young lad with a message from Samuel Adams. The Committee had written briefs of the Tea Party and Paul was requested to immediately deliver them to Hartford, New York and Philadelphia. Young Paul was swiftly out the back door to the stall to ready Paul's horse. Rachel slumped in a chair at the kitchen table, knowing that Paul would be gone in a matter of minutes. The 350 miles to Philadelphia, with frozen drifts on the paths, would keep him away for as many as sixteen days... and Christmas was next week. She could not even lift her eyes to meet Paul's as her disappointment settled in like an unwelcome guest. Her first married Christmas would be spent without her dear husband. Paul engulfed her in an embrace showing his love and concern. He kissed her briefly, as he had all the children and his mother. The family watched as Paul slipped into his surtout, boots and buckled on his metal spurs. He promised to return as promptly as possible and burst out the door into winter.

*~ April 1775 ~*

Rachel slowly grew accustomed to Paul's rapid departures, though, in her opinion, his trips were poorly timed. They interfered with family matters, especially the birth of their first child, Joshua, born last December. Little Joshua was but two days old when Paul was sent to New Hampshire. Rachel did not complain to Paul, or to the children. She missed him terribly, but anticipated his joyous returns.

Anxiety in Boston was a pall in the minds of patriots and British alike. General Thomas Gage, the colonial governor of Massachusetts, had been promoted to Commander in Chief of the British forces in America, a grand title for a man who only controlled redcoats in Boston. General Gage ordered fortifications to be built across "the neck," the single land route out of Boston to the mainland. As hostilities rose, he sent a request to England for 20,000 reinforcements for his troops. In response, England instructed him to arrest Samuel Adams and John Hancock, hoping to subdue "the rowdies."

The Sons of Liberty had taken on the nighttime vigil of spying on the British soldiers to glean information about possible movements or attacks. During a nightly expedition, one of the members learned of a plan for the troops to leave Boston and head to Concord where the colonists had a store of ammunition and weapons. Another member heard of the warrant for Adams' and Hancock's arrest.

Paul knew the British would depart under cover of night, so he met with Robert Newman, a rector in Old North Church. Their belfry was the tallest in Boston and could even be seen from Charleston, across the river. If the British left Boston over the neck, he was to hang one lantern in the tower. If they crossed the Charleston River, two lanterns would be the signal.

Dr. Joseph Warren, a fellow Mason and the interim leader for the Sons of Liberty, gathered the incoming information and decided to send two messengers to warn Adams and Hancock in Lexington. Then they were sent on to alert Concord. The patriots were ready if the troops made a move.

There was a fitful wind blowing the night of April 18ᵗʰ when General Gage ordered the movement to Concord. The familiar knock sounded on the Revere's door late in the night. Paul told Rachel it was business for the Sons of Liberty and was away in an instant. As soon as he was out of doors, he saw two lanterns blazing in the belfry of Old North. The British were crossing by sea!

In the quietness of the night, Rachel prayed for Paul's safety as she drifted back to sleep. As the sun's rays filtered between the shutters of Rachel's window in the morning, she was awakened by the soft coos of baby Joshua in the cradle at the foot of the bed. She wondered why Paul had not returned from the Green Dragon. She called for Paul Jr., and asked him to check if their horse was still in the stall behind the house. Paul Jr. returned in an instant, "Yes, Mum, she's in her stall, but Papa didn't feed her this morning."

"Please see to it, son." Rachel requested. "Your father must be on important business."

All day Rachel wondered where her husband had ventured without his trusted horse. Young Paul went to his father's silversmith shop and learned from fellow apprentices of a battle at Lexington between minutemen and the British. He was breathless after he ran home to tell Rachel the news. That night the sun slid behind the hills and the evening sky darkened to ink, yet no word came from Paul.

It was past noon the following day when Dr. Benjamin Church arrived at the Revere home with grave news. Dr. Church was a member of the Committee of Correspondence. "Mrs. Revere, I'm afraid your husband will not be returning to Boston," he spoke solemnly. "He was arrested two nights ago, but was released unhurt. There was a terrible battle with many wounded. I have returned to Boston to secure medicine for the soldiers and Paul asked that you send him money so that he may board with a family in Cambridge."

Paul's mother gathered a piece of parchment, an ink well and quill and instructed Rachel to write a note to Paul. Meanwhile, Deborah sent Paul Jr. to the shop for the cash box while she collected hidden money from various places throughout the house. Rachel sat at the kitchen table and penned,

> My dear, by Doctor Church I send a hundred and twenty-five pound & beg you will take the best care of yourself & not attempt coming into this towne again & if I have an opportunity of coming or sending out anything or any of the children I shall do it. Pray keep up your spirits & trust yourself & us in the hands of a good God who will take care of us. Tis all my dependence, for vain is the help of man. Adieu my love. From your Affectionate, R. Revere.

Rachel and the family did not hear from Paul again for weeks. News eventually arrived that Paul was employed as an express rider for Massachusetts, and had arranged to house his family in Watertown. During this time, Rachel worked diligently at securing a pass for them to leave Boston. She eventually bribed a British officer with two bottles of beer, a bottle of wine, veal and beef. In return, the family was free to depart. Paul had instructed Paul Jr. to stay behind and secure the business and the house, while Rachel, Deborah and the six children left over the neck in an overflowing cart.

It was early May when Paul was reunited with Rachel and his family. Paul hugged and kissed each one and then repeated the affections a second time. Once again, Rachel sat in amazement, while her animated husband recounted his ride of April 18th.

"Dr. Warren sent me across the Charleston River to Lexington and to Concord. I alerted all the houses I passed that the regulars were approaching. I dodged two mounted soldiers just outside Charleston Common. I rode like the wind, my love," Paul bragged, as Rachel adored him with her shining dark eyes. "It was midnight when I arrived at Reverend Clarke's home to warn Sam and John to be off. You should have seen John's Aunt, Lydia Hancock, fly into high hysterics at the news, shaking her hands and running in tiny circles. She would have fainted from fright if John had not settled her." He laughed at the thought.

"William Dawes was also sent to warn John and Sam, and he got through over the neck. When he arrived in Lexington, the warning was sounding for the minutemen to assemble on the green. There were repeated gunshots, beating of drums and the ringing of bells. As soon as Dawes rested his horse, we were off to Concord, joined by a fine young doctor named Samuel Prescott. Shortly after, we were surrounded by sentry, but Dr. Prescott is such an excellent rider that he jumped a stone wall and was off. I made for the woods, but was overtaken and forced to dismount. While the soldiers questioned me, Dawes escaped and ventured on to Concord behind the doctor."

"Did they harm you, dear?" Her eyes scanned his body for evidence.

"One of the soldiers rapped me on the head with the butt of his rifle." His hand rose to touch the still tender spot. "But I'm fine, Rachel."

"The redcoats heard the commotion in Lexington and hastened away, leaving me to walk to town. I arrived at the Clarke parsonage around 3:00 a.m. and you will not believe what I found!" Paul hesitated, waiting for Rachel to guess. She did not utter a word, so he continued. "Sam and John were still there, arguing over whether or not they should leave!"

"I hurried them off in a carriage while the battle began on the green. It was horrible, Rachel. There were 75 militia against hundreds and hundreds of British troops. Eight of our men fell dead and ten more were wounded before dispersing." Paul sobered as he reported of the battle.

"The British moved on to Concord, where they met 300 patriots and were forced to withdraw. As they marched back to Boston, colonists fired at them from behind barns, bridges and trees. Many British were also killed. It was a horrific scene."

"That night, I feared that I might never see you again. I am relieved to have you, mother and the children here safely." Paul admired his wife as he held her. "Don't fret, my dear. You will soon feel secure in the countryside away from the troops in Boston."

Rachel rested in her husband's arms at his reassuring words before turning her attention to settling her family in their new surroundings.

*~ Epilogue ~*

Paul and Rachel Revere had eight children of their own, five who lived to adulthood. Together, they raised all eleven. Paul never did receive the monies or the letter Rachel sent with Dr. Church, as the doctor turned out to be an informant for General Gage. Following his midnight ride, Paul was in the Massachusetts militia as a lieutenant colonel of artillery. He started a powder mill to aid the colonists in the Revolutionary War. After the war, he continued to manufacture gold and silver wares. Along with this, he also opened the first copper plating mill in America, built a foundry where metal bells were cast, and opened a small hardware store. Paul retired from active work at 76 years old, still surrounded by his children, grandchildren, and great-grandchildren. Rachel passed away at the age of 68, five years before Paul died, in 1818, at the age of 83. The *Boston Intelligence* carried an obituary for Paul stating, "Seldom has the tomb closed upon a life so honorable and useful."

To this day, each year on April 18th, two lanterns are hung in the Old North Church by a descendant of either Paul Revere or Robert Newman, to commemorate his famous ride.

### About the Author:

 Linda Ann Crosby is an author, speaker, wife and homeschooling mother of three. She has written a devotional book for moms, encouraging them to laugh in the midst of it all. She has also contributed to unit studies on Africa and Indians for the Konos curriculum. She leads a mentoring ministry at her church and escapes to scrapbooking retreats whenever possible. Linda and her husband Rick spent the first ten years of their marriage in Northern Canada but have made their home in Phoenix, Arizona since 1997.

*I dedicate this story to Admiral Horatio Lord Nelson who made this all possible. And to Josh, Joey, Matt, and Ryan who have been very supportive and encouraging to me, I dedicate this story to these good friends as well. - Andrew*

*To family and friends who have played parts in making dreams come true for us, we thank you. The One who gives dreams and makes us who we are has given us all dreams and hopes that ring in our ears and make our hearts pound. Don't let go of your dreams. Don't let what happens in this life tell you what will be. He wants you to feel the thrill of seeing your dreams come true. Keep dreaming, keep trusting in Him to make things come to be. And so, we dedicate this story to you, with the feel of salt-air on our cheeks, the wind in our hair, and huge smiles on our faces. - Tracey and Andrew*

# Admiral Lord Nelson

Victory!

1758 - 1805

*by Andrew and Tracey Boynton*

Europe
1800

Atlantic
Ocean

SCANDINAVIA

DENMARK

ENGLAND

Burnham Thorpe

London

Copenhagen

RUSSIA

Rhine R.

Paris

FRANCE

The Alps

The Pyrenees

Toulon

Danube R.

Black Sea

Corsica

SPAIN

Sardinia

The Apennines

Rome

Naples

Cape
Trafalgar

Palermo

Sicily

Athens

Crete

Mediterranean Sea

AFRICA

Alexandria

0            500 Miles

0            800 Km

EGYPT

# Admiral Lord Nelson

## Victory!

*by Andrew and Tracey Boynton*

### *Adventures in the Navy - 1805*

Horatio Nelson sat in his cabin aboard the HMS *Victory*, toying with the chelengk, on his old battered admiral's hat. The chelengk was a beautiful diamond turban ornament made in the shape of a flower with thirteen rays coming out of it. Each ray represented a ship that Nelson had taken in the Battle of the Nile. It was a gift given to him by Sultan Selim III of Turkey. Looking at it caused him to reflect on past battles, both won and lost, as well as sailors he had fought beside. It had been years since he had joined His Majesty's Royal Navy. He could imagine no other kind of life; but then, he could not have imagined this life either.

When he began his naval career as a twelve year-old coxswain in 1771, he would never have presumed to imagine that one day he would stand as Commander-in-Chief of the Mediterranean, let alone be honored as Admiral Lord Viscount, Duke of Bronte, Knight of the Order of Bath to list just some of his titles. Besides these, he would also have the distinction of losing an arm, an eye, and having a scar that crossed his forehead, each wound inflicted from a different battle.

Nelson placed the hat on his ornate weather-beaten desk with his only arm. He was ready for his evening meal, but he never wasted time. As he waited for his tea to arrive, he glanced at the nautical map that lay outspread across his desk. A young midshipman knocked on the door to his cabin. Nelson looked up from his maps and charts.

"Come in," Horatio said in a commanding voice.

"Lord Nelson? I've brought your tea."

The young man entered the room carrying a large oak tray. The scent of roasted chicken, potatoes and root vegetables wafted into the room with him. There was also a bowl that contained some apples and a teapot covered with a cozy. The young man set down the tray and took his time putting things in order before he straightened. He nodded quickly at Lord Nelson and began to walk toward the door, then stopped as though he had forgotten something.

Nelson looked up from his meal. "Yes? Is there something else?"

The midshipman started to shake his head as his courage waned, but then, gathering his bravery, he stood at attention and in a strong voice asked, "Sir, might I be so bold as to ask you to relate some of your adventures, Sir?"

Nelson peered at the young man with his one seeing eye. "I look at you, lad, and I see myself as a young boy. I am feeling nostalgic today, so I will tell you a tale or two. I feel I have had a wonderful life. I have a lovely wife and a brave stepson who has grown up and has fought beside me for king and country. God has blessed me, and so I fight for His glory."

"I began much like you probably did, without much fanfare or excitement. I was born in a small rectory in Burnham Thorpe in the English countryside of Norfolk, which sits on the edge of the North Sea. My uncle was a naval hero, my father still is the finest vicar in Norfolk, and my great-grand uncle was the first Prime Minister of England. My family has been God-blessed and is God-fearing, too. When I was twelve, I helped my uncle in the navy. I discovered from the very start, though, that I suffer from chronic seasickness, much to my horror. I have battled it as much as any enemy I have ever come across and it has always fought hard, but I have never let it defeat me. I had a good naval beginning, but it almost ended before it really began because I was foolhardy and rebellious and disobedient to my captain. So that you can learn from my foolishness and need not make the same foolish mistake, this is the tale I will tell you from my life..."

"When I was fifteen I was aboard the HMS *Carcass* as we sailed into the bitter cold of the Arctic. We were headed to the North Pole in hopes of finding the long sought northern passage to India. Another midshipman of my same age convinced me of his idea to hunt for polar bear, and so we left the ship without permission. We came across a polar bear while we were still within sight of our ship at anchor, but my musket didn't fire. The dampness had kept it from lighting! As the angry polar bear advanced, my friend turned back and ran to the rowboat. I wasn't about to give up my prize, though. So with a useless musket as my only weapon, I began beating the bear about the head. I was causing him some injuries, and I like to think I would have ultimately defeated my enemy, but a shot was fired from the ship and the noise frightened off the polar bear. I lost the prize that day, but I probably gained my life. When I got back to the *Carcass*, I had Captain Lutwidge to face. He was as angry as that polar bear had been. Captains do not take kindly to young midshipmen leaving the ship without permission to do dangerous and foolish things. 'What the devil were you doing out there?' he asked. 'Sir, I wanted that white bear hide to send back to my father in England,' I replied."

"Fortunately, I was not flogged, which is what most captains would have done to young sailors such as we. Instead, he gave me a stern lecture, and from that day on, he would tell that story to his guests at every dinner party he held."

Horatio ate some of the tempting roast chicken from the tea tray. "Thank you for letting me reminisce, but you are probably needed up on deck."

The young man nodded with a smile. "Thank you, sir. I'll never forget this, sir—never! Thank you. Good evening."

Nelson watched the young midshipman walk to the door. This time of reverie, of remembering himself as a young boy, had not kept Nelson from what was uppermost in his mind. The HMS *Victory* was anchored off the coast of Spain waiting to meet Napoleonic forces once again. Nelson knew that the fight that was to begin shortly after daybreak tomorrow was, without doubt, the most important fight of his life. How would it play out? As he looked over at his admiral's hat, he saw the diamond chelengk that adorned it. In his mind's eye he could picture each ship that the thirteen diamond rays represented. They were Napoleon's finest ships of the line, and when Nelson had overtaken them all in battle it was one of Horatio's proudest moments. He had come up against Napoleon and his navy many other times, but seven years ago, Nelson had prevented Napoleon from taking his war against the British to India. Yes, it had been a merry chase around the Mediterranean, and he could remember it as though it were yesterday.

116

*Where are the French?* - 1798

The HMS *Vanguard* had sailed so close to the Toulon harbor that they could see the sails of the French war ships that were obviously preparing for something of magnificent proportions. Then, under cover of night, the French moved their entire fleet out and away. When morning light came, they were gone. The harbor had been full with 13 massive ships of the line (warships that were powerful enough to take their place in a battle line with guns on two, three and sometimes four decks) and 400 frigates (smaller ships that carried all their guns on a single deck), troop-ships and supply craft. Napoleon's flagship *L'Orient* was a 120 gun, 2000-ton ship, the largest fighting ship of its time, and it had sailed past the Vanguard without so much as a ripple in the water. Nelson had lost the French and now they had the entire Mediterranean ocean to search!

Nelson was furious, but he somehow felt certain they had gone to Alexandria in Egypt. Eventually, ten more English ships arrived and together they and the *Vanguard* set off to Alexandria, where Nelson hoped to find the French fleet anchored off the coast. Disappointment was what awaited Nelson and his men in Alexandria. They didn't stay long, but set a course along the Egyptian coast. This time of sailing around in search of the missing French could have been a humiliating time for a leader, but instead, Nelson bonded with his young captains, many of whom were his same age or younger, and later called them his "band of brothers."

They left Egypt and sailed toward the island of Crete. They went on to Sicily, but found the French were not there, so they decided to go to Greece. In a small town on the coast of Greece, the governor told them that fishermen had seen 400 French ships going by just a few days earlier headed in the direction of Egypt. Could it be Alexandria after all?

The *Vanguard* set sail with new energy toward Egypt. When they arrived in the harbor there was a bit of a shock. Transport ships to move soldiers were anchored, but there were no warships. Was it possible? Had they yet again missed their elusive prey? Nelson ordered the fleet to prepare to set sail again and sat down for the midday meal. Half way through the first bite of his buttered roll, a captain opened the oaken door.

"Sir! We've received word from the guard of the watch that the French fleet is anchored in the Bay of Aboukir, eight leagues east of the city!"

"Excellent! Cast off! We will head there immediately!"

Meanwhile in the bay, Admiral Brueys, leader of the French fleet, had put the frigates in a line with the ships' guns pointing east. The man in the Crow's Nest shouted down, "The English are coming! They're leaving Alexandria!"

Brueys smiled, "Nelson won't attack this late in the evening and in this shallow water. We will escape tonight!"

Nelson knew that a night attack was dangerous and naval custom of the time discouraged night fighting, but he was not about to let them escape again! At six in the evening, Horatio could see the French and to his amazement, he saw that his enemy's fleet was still anchored and lined up in a row. This would make for an easy attack. Nelson divided his fleet in two, sending one half to the port side of the frigates, and the other half to their starboard side. In this way, his enemy's ships were sandwiched in between his own.

On his command, the gun ports on all Nelson's ships were opened and his powder monkeys readied the cannons.

"Fire!"

Before the French knew what hit them, cannon balls were ripping through hull and deck and the smell of gunpowder filled the air.

118

Brueys started yelling orders and anchors were pulled up. Those cannons that were undamaged were readied and he gave the order to fire back.

The French were in disarray, but they fought furiously. In the second hour of the battle, a cannon ball crashed through the railing on *L'Orient*, and hit Brueys directly, causing him to lose both of his legs. He commanded his men to prop him up on the quarterdeck so he could give orders as long as he was able. "Load the guns, and quick! Hurry! Hurry!" Soon after, another cannonball hit the quarterdeck and killed him. A fire started on *L'Orient*, which found its way to the powder kegs. There was a great explosion and the ship sank. The explosion was so loud it was heard in Alexandria.

It took another nine hours for the battle to finish. In the end, four frigates were sunk in addition to *L'Orient*, seven were captured and two escaped. In all, 800 French souls were lost. English gunners fell asleep next to their cannons from sheer exhaustion. Nelson escaped with only a deep gash across his forehead from flying debris. The Battle of the Nile went down in history as one of the most spectacular French defeats of the Napoleonic wars. But Nelson knew he could not rest on his laurels. There would be more battles ahead. Napoleon had an ever-watchful eye and a tactical mind; surely he was planning some new disaster to bring upon England. Nelson, too, would be waiting and watching, ready to match whatever Napoleon would dish out.

As Nelson sat in his cabin with memories flooding his mind, he was surprised at the vividness of them all. If he closed his eyes he could hear the guns and smell the gunpowder. That smell was maybe the strongest memory trigger of all. Somehow it never seemed to fade. Yes, it had seemed like yesterday, but there had been many battles since the Battle of the Nile. Many good men who had fought and lived that day were now gone. Nelson stood to stretch his legs. He took a sip of tea, but it had gone cold. He glanced at the tea tray. Nothing looked appealing. He wasn't hungry. He wasn't anxious. He was somehow melancholy. What was making his mind return to these times from the past? As he moved toward the map on his desk, he walked by the table next to the wall. A small, simple vase that rested there caught his attention. It reminded him of the Roman vases that Sir William Hamilton, Ambassador to Naples, had collected and obsessed over. Most of those vases lay on the bottom of the Tyrrhenian Sea, never making it very far out of the harbor of Naples when the Hamiltons and the Neapolitan royal family had escaped from Naples with Nelson's help. He wondered at the thought. It seemed a strange memory to come to mind today, yet he could remember it all so clearly. God had surely sailed with him during those days.

## To Save a Royal Family - 1798

Captains Capel and Hoste, from Nelson's crew, were sent ahead with news of the victory of the Battle of the Nile to London. On their way to London, they stopped in Naples, Italy, to rest and bring the good news. When Sir William, the English Ambassador to Naples, and his wife, Lady Emma Hamilton, heard what had happened at the Battle of the Nile, they were very pleased. It took a few more weeks before the HMS *Vanguard* arrived in Naples for much needed repairs, and by that time, everyone knew of Nelson's great victory. He was greeted with great honor and enthusiasm by crowds, and Lady Emma prepared a victory ball in the Palazzo Sessa for seventeen hundred guests to celebrate the battle and Nelson's 40th birthday. Sultan Selim III gave Nelson the chelengk to commemorate the victory at the Battle of the Nile that evening. It was an incredible night.

Although life in Naples seemed lighthearted and carefree, there was trouble brewing beneath the surface. King Ferdinand, the king of Naples, was also king of Sicily and he couldn't decide what he wanted to do about this war that was raging all over Europe. Should he remain neutral or join with the English and fight Napoleon? His Queen, Maria Carolina, hated France for beheading her sister, Marie Antoinette. After much persuasion, she convinced him to try to take back Rome from Napoleon. Ferdinand sent his army into battle, and they entered Rome on November the 29th with very little resistance. The French army fled from Rome without a fight. It seemed to be a tremendous triumph for Ferdinand, but it did not last long.

Ferdinand and his men were forced to flee Rome a few days later as French reinforcements bore down on them and retook the city. Arriving in Naples, Ferdinand and his men warned of an impending attack. Ferdinand hid and his men scattered in fear. Peasants held protests outside the King's grand palace, demanding he muster an army to protect Naples, so Ferdinand appealed to Nelson.

"I need help! I have no intention of gathering an army! Save me!" He had decided to return with his family to Sicily and needed a clandestine escape from Naples. He had no desire to stay and fight for his people and perhaps risk injury or death to himself or his family. The King was desperate.

Nelson answered him. "I don't believe you can leave Naples with a thousand paupers waiting outside your door. The Turkish ambassador, Selim is having a party on December the 21st. Perhaps that evening I can get you out of Naples and take you to Sicily."

On the night of the party, it was pouring rain. Carriages took the Ambassador and Mrs. Hamilton, Nelson and the Neapolitan royal family to the party. A servant greeted them at the large doors but quickly directed them toward a tall dark-skinned man dressed in a white coat, white trousers and a scarlet fez.

"Greetings effendis! I am Ambassador Selim of Turkey!" He then introduced himself to the youngest members of the royal family. "You are most welcome to my home!" He walked them through the rooms lined with bookshelves and others filled with beautiful treasures from his homeland and toward the tables filled with flowers and food. Men walked through the enormous house serving appetizers to all the guests. When the time seemed appropriate, they said their goodbyes to the Ambassador. However, rather than exiting through the front door, Nelson led the Hamiltons and the royal family out the back door to carriages that were waiting to take them to the harbor and the HMS *Vanguard*, which was repaired and ready to sail. Sir William had been unwilling to leave Naples without the obsession of his life, a collection of ancient Roman vases. So another carriage set out for the harbor that evening filled with his vase collection.

The rainstorm that had begun the night grew into an unabating gale, and the *Vanguard* was forced to stay in the harbor for two days. When the weather cleared and the ship was finally able to set sail for Sicily on the 23rd of December, the peasants discovered their king had abandoned them to the approaching French troops. The King of Naples was horrified to see hundreds of peasants in small rowboats, rowing toward the *Vanguard*. They knew their King was aboard ship and they did not intend to let him go without a fight.

"Your Majesty! How could you think of abandoning your own kingdom and your humble followers? Please, help us! Please! Please, do not abandon your good people!"

There was no response from Ferdinand. The HMS *Vanguard* lifted anchor and started to move out of the harbor.

"Please! We beg you!" yelled the peasants.

Their cries were met with silence. The people of Naples felt their king was cowardly as he fled from the frightening days that were surely coming.

Aboard the Vanguard, Sir William's anxiety over his vases was abidingly evident. They were onboard another ship on their way to England, while he and his wife were headed to Sicily. Though good weather was predicted for the holiday season, he was distraught regarding the vases' safety. As they embarked, he declared across the water, "Alright. Let us go! Oh, have a happy Christmas, my beautiful vases!" His 'beautiful vases' didn't have a happy Christmas. Soon after they left the port at Naples, what should have been good weather erupted into violent storms that lasted four long days. The ship carrying the vases sank on Christmas Day of 1798, taking them to the bottom of the Tyrrhenian Sea. Horatio and the youngest prince, Carlo Alberto, were horribly ill from the heaving and rocking of the boat.

On the second day into their journey, on the 24th of December, a terrified midshipman ran to Nelson screaming to be heard over the roar of the monstrous waves. "Lord Nelson! We've gotten a hole during the tempest! We're sinking! There must be a Jonah on board! Say prayers, for we shall all die! O Lord, my God! Save us from--" Those were the last words the man spoke as a sudden wave pulled him into the sea. Nelson had seen more blood and horrors of war in a few years than most men see in a lifetime, but this bizarre incident horrified him. The man was killed by the waves before finishing his prayer. Had God forsaken them after all? Was it possible? The ship was going to sink if something didn't happen quickly!

He could hear Queen Maria screaming. The prince had begun

having terrible convulsions as the seasickness became more than his body could take. Lady Emma and the Queen were panicked because they had no idea how to help the poor child. Sir William was no help to anyone. He was so frightened that he did not move. Although Horatio himself was extremely ill, he knew he could not give in to his seasickness. He had to do something to save the ship. With a power not his own, he shouted to the crew, "Block up the hole! Do something, men! You can do it! Do not fail me! Do not fail our glorious king, and never fail England or God!"

God had not forsaken them. He gave them the strength to keep the ship floating until December 26th when the HMS *Vanguard* landed at Palermo, the capital of Sicily. It was truly God's hand at work. Though all the others survived, sadly, Prince Carlo Alberto succumbed during the treacherous voyage across the Tyrrhenian Sea. Nelson ran his fingers across the rim of the small vase that had originally caught his attention and brought the memory to mind. God had always sailed with him. Even when he could not see His hands at work, he knew that God was there. Was that what he was supposed to remember this day? Was he supposed to remember that God was always beside him? Even when he could not see God's hands at work. . . . A smile flickered across his face as he remembered a time when not being able to see had indeed worked to his advantage.

### The Right to be Blind - 1801

In 1801 it seemed like a new war had begun. Russia had been an enemy of France during the whole war. Suddenly, however, Tsar Paul declared war on England, and successfully persuaded his Scandinavian neighbors, Denmark, Sweden and Norway to commit to "Armed

Neutrality" (the idea of being prepared to use force if a country feels threatened). The British Empire saw this move as supporting France and it was unacceptable to them. The British government sent Sir Hyde Parker and his British fleet to the area to compel Denmark and Norway into withdrawing from their pact. Nelson also went as second in command under Parker. Admiral Hyde Parker was higher ranked than Nelson, but they needed Nelson's expertise in battle. Parker hadn't had much recent battle experience and was terribly slow to move to action. When the fleet made its way up the coast of Norway in March they found severe winter gale conditions. It took them two days to round Norway and enter the Sound, the waterway between Denmark and Sweden. They decided the best thing to do was to anchor, wait, and plan their attack. Nelson scouted the Danish-Norwegian fleet and even sent out one of his captains in a small boat at night to get accurate readings of the shoreline and water depths. It was the first time Nelson had been afforded so much time to study an enemy before battle.

On the morning of the attack, Nelson boarded his ship, the HMS *Elephant*, and led a squadron of 11 ships of the line and 7 frigates. Parker was in command of the HMS *London* and led 7 ships. Nelson had a detailed plan for each of his ships and frigates. It was complex and involved every ship. By eight in the morning on April 2nd, the captains had their orders and the fleet set sail by half past nine. Three ships did not make it into the action. One could not sail around a shoal, and two others ran aground on the Middle Ground, an area that had been mapped on one of the reconnaissance missions but was somehow misjudged that day. Admiral Parker began to worry when three hours into the intense battle he was still fighting wind and not close enough to where he was supposed to be. From his vantage point, it looked as though the British force was making no impact on the Danish-Norwegian fleet. He felt

Lord Nelson

that he should give Nelson the opportunity to quit if it was needed. Parker turned to his flag-captain and gave the order to show the signal discontinue action.

"If he is in a condition to continue the action successfully, he will disregard it; if he is not, it will be an excuse for his retreat and no blame can be imputed to him." Parker told one of the captains standing near him watching the battle off in the distance.

On board the *Elephant*, Nelson had no intention of discontinuing action. The smile that had crept onto his face at the memory of that day was because of what he did next. Nelson remembered turning to Captain Foley, his flag-captain and saying to him, "You know, Foley, I have only one eye. I have a right to be blind sometimes." He then put his telescope to his blind eye, and said, "I really do not see the signal!"

It took three more hours before most of the Danish firing ended, and the battle wasn't truly over until half past four. The British fleet had the victory that day, but they suffered stunning losses, both in ships and men, with 1000 killed or wounded. There also were tremendous casualties for the Danish and Norwegians. They lost ships and nearly 2000 men killed or wounded. Even after such devastation, the Danish government agreed only to a 14-week truce. The Battle of Copenhagen had been one of the bloodiest naval battles of the Revolutionary and Napoleonic wars. Nelson had always been a self-confidant leader. He knew how to lead and trusted the plans he put into action. While at times it may have appeared that he was reckless, more often he was revolutionary in the way he fought. He changed the way naval wars were waged.

Yes, the Battle of Copenhagen had been a hard-fought, hard-won battle. But he needed to stop looking behind and start focusing on what lay ahead. What would tomorrow bring? Nelson and his men had been on the HMS *Victory* for weeks, many of them here by Cadiz, Spain at Cape Trafalgar. Finally, tomorrow, it was all going to happen. Is that why he had been having such a day of remembrances? Was it because he was on the eve of such a decisive battle that these memories came to him unbidden? There was much to do at early light, and it was time for bed. Nelson's mind was still a flurry of past battles, old conversations and thoughts of dear friends.

"I need to settle my thoughts or I'll never sleep tonight," he said out loud to no one in particular. "Lord, help me to sleep so that I can bring a victory for you and for England." He straightened things on his desk, readied himself for the night and was soon settled into his bed. He leaned across the downy coverlet and blew out the light. His breathing slowed and light snoring began.

*Committed to Him Who Made Me - October 21ˢᵗ 1805*

As Nelson walked through his cabin in the early morning light, he knew that he was about to fight the most important battle of his life. Napoleon was threatening to send his French fleet into the British Channel, and Nelson was not about to let that happen. The HMS *Victory* and 26 other British ships of the line were prepared to meet a combined French and Spanish fleet in battle. Nelson stopped, turned and walked to his desk. He searched it until he found his ink and quill. He opened his logbook as a look of thoughtfulness crossed his face. He opened the pages and wrote:

"May the Great God, whom I worship, grant to my country, and for the benefit of Europe in general, a great and glorious victory; and may no misconduct in any one tarnish it; and may humanity after victory be the predominant feature in the British Fleet. For myself, individually, I commit my life to Him who made me, and may His blessing light upon

128

my endeavours for serving my country faithfully. To Him I resign myself and the just cause which is entrusted to me to defend. Amen. Amen. Amen." Horatio Nelson, Vice Admiral of the White, H.M.S. *Victory*, 21st October 1805.

Nelson wanted to encourage his men by sending a flag signal that was to read England Confides That Every Man Will Do His Duty. His intent was for them to know that he believed in them and that England believed in them. The sailor who was to send up the flags asked if he could use a different word for "confides" because it was long when written in flags. He was given permission and changed the word to "expects". So the famous message was sent as England Expects That Every Man Will Do His Duty. Some of the men thought Nelson believed they had not done their duty before and they became disheartened. It was disappointing that a message that was sent to encourage the men was twisted and brought discouragement to Nelson's men on the brink of such an important battle. History would call the battle fought that day, "The Battle of Trafalgar."

When Nelson stepped onto *Victory*'s quarterdeck, he surprised Captain Hardy. Nelson was in full dress uniform and with all of his medals and decorations showing proudly. This was most definitely not the typical dress of the commander in charge of a ship going into battle. Captain Hardy was stunned and stood quietly for a moment before finally managing to find the ability to speak.

"My Lord! It will be quite dangerous to wear all your medals into the battle! Perhaps, you should consider wearing an ordinary navy coat? If you wear all your medals, the French sharp shooters will surely know who you are and shoot at you!"

"I'm not afraid to show the enemy who I am!" Nelson replied

stubbornly. He was going to fight beside his men, as he always did, and in his finery. To God be the Glory!

### Epilogue - *A Hero Remembered* - 1805

The Battle of Trafalgar was a great victory for England. The French forces were beaten back, but more importantly, Napoleon's plans to invade England were destroyed. France suffered such losses that it was no longer a naval power, which ensured that the British navy was the dominant force on the seas.

With the battle belonging to England, there should have been much celebration aboard the HMS *Victory* on the evening of October the 21st, but the men of the British fleet were in mourning. Their Commander, Lord Horatio Nelson, was dead. A French sharpshooter aboard the *Redoubtable* had killed him. Before he died he was told that England had the victory, and so he closed his eyes for the last time, proud of his men.

Typically, sailors were buried at sea. Nelson, however, was so loved and respected, that his body was preserved in alcohol and guarded day and night by members of his crew until the shattered hulk of the HMS *Victory* could bring him back to England for a state funeral. The funeral was very elaborate and lasted for five days, from January 5 to 9, 1806. He was greatly loved by the people of England and it showed by the incredible number of people who came out to see his funeral procession as it moved from the river to the streets. There was a black barge that carried Nelson's body down the River Thames from Greenwich and was met by a funeral cart (made to look like the HMS *Victory*) that brought him through the streets of London to St. Paul's Cathedral. Lord Nelson was buried in a coffin made of wood taken from the mast of *L'Orient*, the French ship of the line, and Napoleon's flagship, that was blown up at the Battle of the Nile in 1798. Later this coffin was placed inside a gilded casket with ornate decorations celebrating Nelson's life and victories.

England chose to show their love and gratitude for Lord Nelson in 1829 by creating Trafalgar Square in the heart of London. At the center of the square is Nelson's Column, a 185-foot high column with a 17-foot statue of Lord Nelson at the top. The column is covered in plaques that commemorate Nelson's battles. Nelson's Column was seen as such a symbol of British pride and victory that Hitler never allowed that area of London to be bombed during WWII. Hitler was certain that he would ultimately have victory in England and he wanted to take Nelson's Column back to Berlin as a prize. He did not have his victory, he did not get his prize, and Nelson's Column stands where it originally stood. Lord Admiral Horatio Nelson, considered by many the greatest naval commander of all time, stands forever vigilant, keeping watch over his fleet docked in the harbor.

*About the Authors:*

Andrew is fourteen and looking forward to beginning high school in the fall. He is a confirmed Anglophile and first visited Britain when he was ten. He saw Trafalgar Square and Nelson's Column in person and hopes to visit the U.K. again soon. In fact, his heart's desire is to attend Oxford University's Merton College, where one of his favorite authors,

J.R.R. Tolkien, taught. He loves history and reading fantasy books. Though this is the first work Andrew has had published, he is currently working on two fantasy novels, *The Caves of Death* and *The Darkling Forest*, which he hopes to publish someday.

Tracey has been married for 19 years to Tim, a pastor, and is mother to three children: Andrew, Luke, and Kennan. She is involved with many ministries at her church and in the community. A great portion of her time, however, is spent in taking care of the special needs of two of her children. Andrew and Kennan both have a rare, degenerative neuromuscular disease called Friedreich's Ataxia. In Andrew's case, it has affected his ability to walk, write, type, and do many simple daily activities most people take for granted. Working on this story with Andrew was an incredible experience and was the chance for her to be part of making one of his dreams come true.

*To my beautiful and precious granddaughters: Abigail Elizabeth, Lauren Olivia and Trinity Grace. How I pray that you will grow up to be virtuous women, serving others in joy as serving Christ. Always remember, dear ones, that children are a blessing, not a burden. And always serve Christ with your gifts!*
*Love, Your Grandma Akins*

# Catherine Ferguson

Really, *Really* Free!

1774 - 1859

by Karla Kay Akins

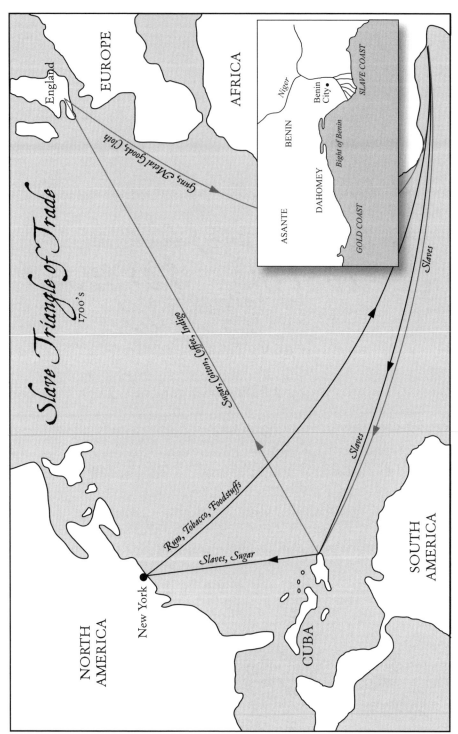

Slave Triangle of Trade
1700's

EUROPE

England

Guns, Metal Goods, Cloth

Sugar, Cotton, Coffee, Indigo

AFRICA

NORTH
AMERICA

New York

Rum, Tobacco, Foodstuffs

Slaves, Sugar

CUBA

Slaves

Slaves

SOUTH
AMERICA

Niger

BENIN

Benin
City

ASANTE

DAHOMEY

SLAVE COAST

Bight of Benin

GOLD COAST

© 2007 Terri Johnson

# VI

# Catherine Ferguson

## Really, *Really* Free!

*by Karla Kay Akins*

"Judge not of virtue by the name
Or think to read it on the skin;
Honor is white and black the same—
The stamp of glory is within."
--Rev. Lewis Tappan, 1857

**1782 – New York City**

"Mamma!!  Mammaaaaaaa!!"

Eight-year-old Catherine Williams cried at the top of her lungs as she clung to her mother in the heat of an early summer day.  Her eyes burned and her face was soaked with angry tears.

"Don't leave me, Mama!  Don't leave me!  Mama! Mamaaaaaaaaa!"

A large, ugly white man grabbed at Catherine and tried to pull her from her mother.  Before he could tear her away, her mother, Hannah

Williams, knelt before her baby girl and laid her scarred hands on her head.

"Lawd, I gib you dis baby girl. Please, Lawd, take care o' my baby. Take care o' her and let her know You."

Before Hannah could pray more, a burly man reeking of whisky and tobacco grabbed her around the waist and tore her away from her daughter's vice-like grip.

"No, Mama, NO!" Catherine screamed.

"Someone hush that child," Catherine heard the Missus say.

"You are a big girl now," Hannah cried bravely. "You do all that Massa Bruce tell you do. You hear me, Catherine? You be brave. Stop that cryin' now. You are God's now, baby girl, I done gib you to God!"

"Hush up woman and get in that wagon," the white slave trader shouted as he pushed Hannah and slapped her shoulder.

"Don't you hit my Mama!" Catherine cried. She wanted to hurt that slave-trader, but two muscular African slaves held on to her to keep her from the wagon. She fought and kicked with all her might. Mud from New York City's dirt road flew up into her mouth, and landed in her black fuzzy hair. It didn't matter. All that mattered was that she would never see her mother again because Mr. Bruce had sold her to another slave owner.

"No! Nooooo!! Don't take my Mama! Don't take my Mama! Please, please, don't take my Mama! Mamaaaaaaaa, don't leave! Don't leave! Mama! Maaaaaamaaaa!"

The rickety wagon pulled away and turned a far corner as Catherine screamed and thrashed in terror and grief. When the men let go of her she ran to the attic weeping and tearing at her clothes. Bearing more pain than her little body could stand, she curled up on her straw mattress, clung to her mother's apron, and wept.

It would be her apron now. She was only eight, but she had been helping her mother in the kitchen from the time she could walk. Now that her mother was sold, she was the only slave in the house. Perhaps because of the war, her owners could not afford two slaves anymore.

But today, there would be no dish washing and biscuit making in the Bruce house. Today she would stay in the hot, musty attic and listen to the wind serenade her weeping with soulful cries through the cracks in the walls. Today she would close her eyes and pray she would never awake to the pain of being separated from her precious Mama. Instead of washing floors she would weep and let the memories of her mother fill all the painful empty spaces. She would just lie there and concentrate on all the precious moments she had spent at her mother's side: going to church, cooking for the Bruce family, cleaning, doing laundry, going to the market. She would just stay in her little bed of straw and focus on the memory of her mother's voice singing the hymns they learned at the Scottish Presbyterian Church on Cedar Street.

For days Catherine refused to eat or stir. She kept her eyes closed and dreamed of her mother's deep, silky voice telling the stories of how she had run away from her master in Virginia, stowed away on a schooner, and how Catherine was born there. She dreamed about the father she had never known.

"Tell me the story, Mama," she would say, late at night, when only the two of them were awake, putting away the dishes. "Tell me the story of how I was born free."

"Your father was a free man because he became a British Soldier," her mother would whisper. "The British gave slaves their freedom if they would fight with them. He was going to meet me in Virginie."

"But he didna come?" Catherine would ask.

"That's right, baby girl, he didna come."

"But I did, I come, didn't I, Mama?"

Her mother would laugh softly.

"You, baby girl, you wouldna wait ta be born. When I ran away from da Massa and got on that ship, I was all alone in the belly of dat big schoonuh."

"The *Morning Glory*," Catherine would whisper with wonder.

"Yes, it were a grand ol' ship, baby girl. And you came. I was hidin' down in da belly ub dat big ol' ship. And under da the tobacco leaves, by da sugar and da cotton you was born. My own little Catherine Williams. You was born free."

That was Catherine's favorite part – the being born free part. Her eyes would get large with wonder at the feeling it gave her to know she was really free.

"But when we gots to Virginie, da slave man find me down there in dat ship and sell me and you to Massa Bruce."

Sometimes, after hard days of working with hands chapped and bleeding, and their feet sore and bruised from walking in the ice and snow, her mother would hold her and rock and weep: "I so sorry, baby girl. I so sorry I wuz not strong enough to run after yew wuz born. But I gib you to God. You iz Hiz ta do wid what He wants ta."

A body can only sleep for so long, and finally, after days on her little straw bed in that sweltering attic, Catherine opened her eyes and sobbed into her mother's apron until tears would come no more.

1784-1785

It was Catherine's favorite day. It was the day she took Little Massa and Little Miss to catechism at Mrs. Graham's house.

"You sit by the backdoor, Catherine," the kind Mrs. Graham said warmly.

"Missus sez I iz Katy now, Ma'am," Catherine said softly.

"Why on earth?" Mrs. Graham asked.

"She sez Catherine too fine an' elegint a name fer a slave."

Flustered, Mrs. Graham, a fine Scottish lady who did not believe in slavery, tried not to act shocked.

"Katy is a pretty name. It suits you. Now, you just make yourself at home back here. Of course, I wish you could join us up front, but. . ."

"Yessa, Miz Graham," Katy smiled, helping Mrs. Graham through a difficult moment. "I sho do like ta listen to da little 'uns lessons."

The truth was, Katy would have felt ridiculously out of place in her simple slave garments next to the finely dressed students.

Katy had dressed Little Miss in a crisp, long, white linen shift with billowy sleeves and tiny cuffs at the wrists. Over this she wore a dark green bodice with shiny metal buttons. Buttons were a true luxury in colonial New York and most people fastened their clothes with laces. But the Bruce family was a prosperous family who owned a mercantile. While Mrs. Bruce worked in the store, Katy took care of the house, the cooking and the children, and Katy loved dressing them up in their beautiful clothes and sewing for them.

The little girl's skirt had two parts – a long skirt with a short skirt over it. The short skirt had a beautiful decorative trim that Katy had embroidered with skillful fingers to match the trim on the little girl's white cap. Over the two skirts the child wore an apron. Her dainty little goatskin shoes peeked out from underneath her skirt, and Katy was proud of the way the little girl sat so still and mannerly, obediently reciting her catechism.

Little Massa was handsome, too, in his linen shirt and rust-colored doublet with the shiny new buttons. Katy had sewn the buttons on that very morning before anyone else was awake. He wore green breeches that fastened with buttons, and long white stockings held up by the cuffs of his breeches. Katy had shined his leather shoes before she had gone to bed the night before so that he would be presentable, but he had managed to find a mud puddle or two before arriving.

Katy loved to handle and touch the fine clothes between her fingertips and feel the cool smoothness of the silky materials. She would imagine what it must be like to wear such softness on her own skin. All she had to wear was her dress made of osnaburg – negro cloth – nothing more than rough feed sack material. It scratched her skin and felt like burlap. Her shoes, what was left of them, had come used, raggedy, and too big from the cart man. She tucked her feet with the ugly, dirty slippers under her chair, sat straight and tall and repeated every word Mrs. Graham said.

"When I grow up and I iz free," she whispered to herself. "I iz gonna haz myself a school and I iz gonna talk purdy jus' like Miz Graham. Yessa, I gonna talk real purdy-like and wear taffeta and silk."

Far too soon the lessons were over and it was time to take the children home to feed them and put them down for a nap. While they napped she began to prepare supper for the family. She was only eleven, but she moved expertly around the kitchen. And while she cooked, she repeated the lessons she had learned at Mrs. Graham's and thought about God. She wanted desperately to read the words in His book like Mrs. Graham and her students.

After months of catechism lessons at Mrs. Graham's house, Katy finally decided to ask if she could learn to read.

"Excuse me, Master and Mrs. Bruce," she said with perfect English, just like Mrs. Graham one day after supper. "May I have a word with you?"

Master and Mrs. Bruce raised their eyebrows at Katy. She didn't sound like a slave at all. She sounded like she was mimicking them! How dare this mere slip of a slave girl take such liberties!

"Know your place, slave," the Master growled.

Katy looked down and curtsied, clasping her hands in front of her.

"Yessa Massa."

"What is it you want?" he asked, incensed that she would ask anything of him at all.

"Massa, I wanna learn ta read the Good Book."

Master Bruce smirked. "You can't learn to read, don't you know that? Your breed does not have the mental capabilities of learning higher academics. Besides, what use would you have for reading? You don't need to read to cook and clean and tend children. You are getting mighty uppity these days. Remember your place, and don't you forget it, or I will have to remind you."

"You already know more than our children, Katy," the Missus said. "You need not learn any more than that. It will not make you a good slave. If you do as well as your mother, you will do fine. Your mother didn't know how to read, either."

Master and Mrs. Bruce turned on their fancy heels and clicked down the hall, grumbling and shaking their heads.

"They don' know I iz – I am – smart. I am just as smart as they are. And I ain't no breed, neither, I iz a child o' God just like them, too."

Katy mumbled to herself as she scrubbed the floor. The more she thought about how Master Bruce took her mother from her, and how he treated her like a dog, the more she hated him, and the more miserable she became.

Katy attended the Scottish Presbyterian Church every Sunday with the Bruce family as she had done since she was an infant. She sat

143

up in the Negro section of the balcony with her mother's best friend, Dembi. She loved Sundays. On Sundays even the slaves had some of the day off, and she could be with her mother's friends and hear their stories. It brought Katy comfort to have friends who understood the feelings associated with being owned and treated like property.

She adored Pastor Mason and his voice. She closed her eyes and imagined pictures in her head when he read the stories of the Baby Jesus, Mary and Joseph. But her favorite stories were those of little baby Moses in a basket, how his mother wanted him to live and be free, and how a princess made him a prince. Most of all, she was enthralled with the way Moses grew up and set the Hebrew slaves free.

"Maybe someday, there be a Moses for us," she would whisper to Dembi, who would smile and pat her hand in a motherly sort of way.

Today Pastor Mason was talking about another kind of freedom.

"If the Son therefore shall make you free, ye shall be free indeed! We all are slaves to something," he said reverently. "But the Son of God, Jesus Christ, can make you free no matter who you are!"

Reserved, whispered "Amens" were uttered from the slaves in the gallery, and the white folks in the sanctuary began to squirm. Pastor Mason did not believe in slavery, but he did not preach against it, either – at least, not directly.

After church Catherine went with her friends to the Pinkster grounds at the edge of town, up by the African and pauper's burial ground and the pond at the edge of the forest. There, they would eat, dance, and play games. Even white folks would sometimes come to hear the music on the violin, calabashes and flutes. The soulful songs and vigorous dancing delighted Katy, but her favorite time was when the men would whistle low and mournful songs. She would close her eyes and imagine her father whistling the same, and imagine what it would be like to celebrate the Sabbath with both of her parents.

"Who are all these people, Dembi?" she asked her friend one day. "I know we all come from Africa, but we don't all look and talk the same."

Dembi chuckled.

"You right, chile, you right. Jus' like white folks don' look an' talk all da same, we don' neithuh. And jus' like white folks don' all come from the same place, we don' all come from jus' one place neithuh."

"See that man over there on that hogshead playin' the fiddle? Well, him and his brothers, they is from Congo. And Jethro and hiz wife Pinky? They be from a land called Nigeria."

"What about that lady there?" Katy pointed to a lady doing a jig with such vigor sweat flew out of her hair and sprayed her partner.

"Oh, that be Jenny, she be Guinea. An' befoe you start a-askin', I will point out all the others."

Dembi put her arm around Katy and pointed out people from Togo, Senegal, Gambia, Angola, Mali and the Caribbean. Katy had heard of all of these, but she was still learning everyone's names and roots.

"And Mende," Katy said.

"Mende? Now who here is Mende?" Dembi teased.

"You and me, Dembi, you know that."

"Why, I shore iz, I shore iz, and you are too," she laughed. Dembi was a big woman with a big smile, big hands and a big voice. Her laugh carried into the forest and rang against the leaves of the trees. Katy was sure they could hear that beautiful laugh all the way to Africa.

Katy shook uncontrollably as she sat in Pastor Mason's house. It didn't smell like the Bruce house, where the scents of her baking filled it each day. It lacked the prettiness of Mrs. Graham's house, but it was

145

clean and neat. She was shocked at the idea that she was sitting in her Pastor's house! What would happen if Pastor Mason sent her away? Then she would never be free.

"Hello Katy," he said, coming into the room. "I am pleased to see you. My, how you have grown! It seems like just yesterday your dear mother brought you as an infant for the first time to church."

"Yes, sir, I am 14 years old now," she said, hanging her head low. She suddenly felt ridiculous in her fading dress and makeshift shoes.

"What can I do for you, Katy? Does Mister Bruce know you are here?"

"No, Reverend Mason, sir," she said meekly.

"I see," he said softly, sitting across from her. "So what is it? Have you come here to talk to me about your soul?"

Katy looked up at the Pastor with tears in her eyes.

"I want to ask Jesus to make me free, like you said, Reverend Mason. But I have lots of hate in my heart toward Master Bruce, and I don't know if Jesus will forgive me. Do you think He can?"

Pastor Mason took Katy's hands in his and smiled. "I am sure of it," he said, and prayed with young Catherine Williams as she accepted Jesus Christ as her Lord and Savior. Unlike many other churches in the city, Pastor Mason encouraged slaves to come to salvation through Christ. Other churches believed slaves only wanted to convert to Christianity in order to become free of their masters.

"This Sunday, you shall be baptized and take Holy Communion," he said. "Will you be able to come?"

"Yes sir," she said, glowing. "Yes, sir, I will be there."

Word traveled fast that the little slave girl, Katy Williams, was going to be baptized and take communion at the "white folks" church on Cedar Street. No slave or person of color had ever taken communion with the white people before. The Bruce family was embarrassed and went out of town. Even some of the slaves resented Katy "not knowing her place." But Katy bravely made her way up to the front of the church to take communion. All the eyes in the church were on her and Pastor Mason. His kind eyes and outstretched hand strengthened her to be brave.

"I wish Mama could have been here, Dembi," she said later. "I think she would have been proud."

"I know she would have been. Now you iz really free, Katy. Now you iz really, really free."

Katy nodded. It was strange not hating Master Bruce anymore. And Master Bruce himself didn't know how to handle Katy's sweet attitude. And while he resented that she had joined "his" church, it was the first time he had ever seen a true conversion, and it moved even his own cold heart.

"You are going to explode if you eat another cake, John Ferguson," Katy teased, blushing.

"Yo haz da best cakes in New Yawk, Miz Williams, I jus' cain't help myself," John said, gulping down another cake. "They iz like a piece ub heben."

"You has had enough," scolded Dembi. "Go on. You go on and get yo-self some menue[1] or moimoi[2] and leave Miz. Katy 'lone. Go on now." Dembi clucked and put her hands on her hips. "That boy sweet on you, Miz Katy."

"I know," Katy said. "You think he's handsome, Dembi?"

---

[1] A Senegalese cornmeal mush.
[2] Nigerian bean pudding.

Dembi smiled. Yes, he was handsome.

"He be okay far as looks go, but more den dat, Katy, he a good Christian man – and a Mende – and a free man, too."

"Oh I just love Pinkster, don't you Miss Dembi?" Katy giggled. Dembi threw back her head and laughed.

"Pinkster always been a happy time, Katy. Always a good happy time for da Massa and Missus to let us slaves celebrate da Pentecost."

Every year since the Dutch Slave Masters had celebrated Pentecost in the late 1600's, slaves had gathered on Pinkster Hill for three days of freedom from work and to visit with friends and family. Pinkster was also a chance for Katy and her friends to make their own money. Africans, slave and free, sold food native to their homeland in makeshift booths, decorated with flowers. It was during the happy days of Pinkster that Katy learned more about being a Mende, and even more about Africa.

Katy's booth was beautifully decorated. Full, fragrant vines made of pink and lavender azaleas were generously draped on Katy's table and canopy making it one of the prettiest booths at Pinkster. But even without the decorations, Katy's booth would have been busy. Her cakes and pastries were a popular treat at the festival. Other booths sold berries, sassafras bark, beverages, shrimp and oysters. But nobody could match the lightness and flavor of Katy's cakes and tarts.

"It's almost time for the speeches and the stories!" Katy said, covering up her goods with white cotton cloths and closing her booth.

She and Dembi sat on an old raggedy blanket and listened to speeches about freedom, stories about Africa, and songs about the woes of slavery. But Katy loved the stories the best, and she especially liked it when John Ferguson told the story of how he had escaped from the south, hid with the Indians and then swam to freedom from a ship.

When it was time for the shingles dance, four men held a piece of square canvas down on a platform while the dancers performed the "jig," "breakdown," and "double shuffle." Katy was laughing at one of the dancers when she noticed John Ferguson watching her. She blushed and looked down at her hands. She turned away as he walked toward her smiling.

"Miz Williams," he said grinning, "would ya like ta join me foe some a dem spicy fried bananas at da Ghana booth?"

"Why, Mr. Ferguson, wouldn't you rather buy one of my pastries instead?"

John smiled. "Why I shore would, Miz Williams, I shore would."

He took Katy's hand and placed it on his arm. Dembi, irritated, followed them back to the booth.

"We iz closed, John Ferguson, don't know how a body can eat so much cake. You must has hollow logs for legs," Dembi grumbled.

In the evening, John Ferguson and Katy walked alone for a little while as Dembi watched carefully, clucking her tongue and complaining about being in the booth by herself.

"Miz Williams," John said. "I think yew iz a very purdy woman and yew shore do knows how to make cake."

"Why thank-you, Mr. Ferguson. I have been making cake a long time. I have even made some wedding cakes, and I make all the lemon tarts for Mr. Bruce's store."

"I know," he said smiling.

"Have you been buying my lemon tarts at the store, John Ferguson?"

"I has. I has been watching yew a long time, Miz. Williams," he said. "And you sure do talk purdy, too."

Katy trembled. He liked the way she talked! She had worked so hard to sound like a proper lady, and this handsome man had noticed.

"You think you could ever marry a man like me, Miz. Williams?"

"Depends," Katy said.

"Depends on what?"

"Depends on if a man like you loves God, goes to church, and doesn't mind being married to a woman with dreams."

"I iz a man of God, Miz. Williams. Oh, I shore is. What kind a dreams you got?"

"I want to be free so I can start a school for children to learn about Jesus – a school like Mrs. Graham's."

"You read?!"

"No," Katy answered sadly.

"Then how you gonna teach dem chillins?"

"I have memorized all the catechisms and most of the scriptures they need to know. Master Bruce never let me learn to read. You read John Ferguson?"

"No, I shore don't."

"When I get free, I hope I can read," Katy said.

"Me too," John said. "Iffin' you can read as good as you cook, you be the smartest woman in New Yawk, slave or free."

He kissed her on the hand, and Katy felt the happiest she had felt since her mother had gone. The empty spaces inside were filling up and almost overflowed.

1787-1788

"Pastor Mason, I need to start a school."

Pastor Mason looked at the little slave sitting across from him. Katy was one of his favorite parishioners. She was spunky, brave, hardworking, and loved the Lord more than anyone he knew. Her speech was articulate and she sounded as well educated as any of the young people who attended Mrs. Graham's catechism classes.

"I want to start a school to teach the poor and the slave children about Jesus, Reverend Mason. They have no one to tell them."

Pastor Mason was startled. How did someone who had been through so much pain find the strength to dream or even reach out to others? He smiled to himself. He already knew the answer to that question. Of course it was the grace of God that sustained Katy Williams.

"Katy, I think that's a fine idea," he said. But how could she do it as a slave? If only she could be freed.

"I don't know where to have this school," she said. "I am hoping you could help me."

Pastor Mason thought for a moment and then lifted his eyebrows.

"I will ask Mayor Duane if you can clear the old battery barracks."

The battery barracks were located where the Dutch settlers had built a stone fort in 1628. In 1741 it was burned down when the British conquered and rebuilt it to house their soldiers. But George Washington drove them out and the fort was again destroyed. It had been abandoned ever since.

"Do you think he'd really let me?" Katy was encouraged by the idea but then suddenly her shoulders drooped.

"I think so – what's wrong, Katy?"

"Master Bruce – I don't know if my faith is strong enough to believe he would let me start my school. He won't let me learn to read. Will you pray with me that he lets me start my school?"

"Yes, Katy, I will pray, even now." And they bowed their heads together and asked the Lord's favor with Master Bruce. After all, it was God's idea, and it was up to God to see it come to pass.

151

A few weeks later on a night after dinner, Katy decided to ask Master Bruce if she could start a school at the battery barracks.

"You really don't know your place, do you, slave?" he smirked after she asked him.

The words pierced Katy's heart. The Bruce family was the only family she knew. And yet, they weren't her family at all. She loved them dearly, and with the grace of God, was even able to forgive them, but they did not love her in return.

"Master Bruce, I would like your permission to clean up the battery barracks so I can start a Christian school for poor children."

Master Bruce winced at her perfect grammar. It was unnatural to hear a slave talk so well. But then, there wasn't anything typical about Katy. He glared at her for a moment, and then, for no reason that he could imagine, he opened his mouth and spoke.

"You may work at the barracks, but only after all other duties are accomplished and only in the evening, after the children are in bed."

"Yes, Master Bruce," Katy curtsied and she could hardly contain herself. She didn't know how she would accomplish it – but God put "yes" in Master Bruce's mouth! God had not failed her yet!

Katy worked hard day and night. During the day she worked as a slave – toiling before anyone in the Bruce home opened their eyes and long after they closed them at night. Then, she would make her way down to the barracks and begin cleaning. She wanted to make the foul place a real home for the children she wanted to teach.

One day she was working in the Bruce kitchen making teacakes when Mrs. Bruce told her to go to Mrs. Graham's house. She had been baking for Mrs. Graham for the past two years on top of completing all of her duties at the Bruce house and cleaning up the barracks.

"I hope she wants me to make a maple nut cake," Katy thought as she made her way through the muddy streets of New York. She walked with her head high, even though white people avoided her as if she were vermin. They would make wide circles around her because they thought slaves were not equal to them.

"Such Christian charity," Katy thought to herself. "Lord, I forgive them, they know not what they do," she prayed.

She always felt peaceful in Mrs. Graham's house. Delicate doilies and laces graced all the tables, and Katy was fascinated with the blue and black hooked rug under her feet. It must be like walking on pillows all day long, Katy thought.

When Katy entered the house, Mrs. Graham and her daughter, Mrs. Bethune, were sitting poised and proper on a green velvet camelback sofa with mahogany trim having their afternoon tea. Katy was fascinated with their beautiful dresses. Their smooth shiny hair was pulled back in tight braided buns at the base of their necks. She longed to feel the silky tendrils that hung in pretty waves at the sides of their face. Their hands were as soft and white as a baby's. As she entered the room, she smoothed her own frizzy hair, hid her scarred, bent hands and smiled.

"Hello, Katy!" Mrs. Graham stood and greeted Katy warmly with outstretched arms. "I am so glad you could come! Please, won't you join us for tea?"

Katy merely nodded, feeling uncomfortable in her raggedy clothes. But she loved Mrs. Graham and didn't want to disappoint her.

"Yes, ma'am, thank-you," Katy said softly.

"Katy," Mrs. Graham said as she poured the tea. "I have a surprise for you."

She handed Katy her tea and then a piece of paper with words on it that Katy couldn't understand.

"I can't read, Mrs. Graham, what is it?"

153

Mrs. Graham giggled softly and looked at her daughter who also smiled with twinkling eyes.

"Katy, darling, this paper is your freedom. Remember how you've been working for us a few hours each week? Well, in return for your work, we paid Mr. Bruce a down payment on your freedom, and now we have purchased it in full."

"Freedom?" Katy whispered, nearly dropping her teacup. "I'm free?"

Katy thought her heart would never make its way back into her chest. Suddenly the room was spinning, suddenly the birds were singing much louder than before, suddenly, her entire world exploded into tiny colorful pieces. Tears spilled down her cheeks onto her faded calico dress. "I am free," she whispered. "I am free, just like my mother wanted me to be. Free."

She couldn't keep from saying that word over and over as she made her way back to the Bruce house. And when she met Mr. Bruce at the door, she was no longer welcome inside the house – the only home Katy had ever known. Katy was alone on the street. She had no food, no clothes, and nowhere to go except the army barracks where she had been cleaning. She was completely alone in the vast, barren world.

*So this was what it is like to be free*, she thought to herself as she walked to the barracks. You can be free but you can still be hungry. Still, I'd rather be free and hungry than a slave and well fed any day.

Katy curled up on a pile of old canvas and drifted off to sleep, hugging her freedom papers tightly to her chest. And for the first time in her life, she dreamt her dreams as a woman of freedom.

1789-1840

"Katy! Katy where are you? Kateeeeey!"

Katy was hanging laundry on a cold winter morning in March.

Catherine Ferguson

The ocean was restless and loud and the wind brought sprinkles of sea water that landed on Katy's eyelashes and made her hair sparkle. Finally, she heard Dembi hollering for her like a banshee.

"Katy, for heaven's sakes, why don' ya answer when I calls you?" she whined.

"I was hanging laundry. The children last night were extremely dirty!"

Dembi clucked her tongue and shook her head. "Youse canna save da worl' Katy. Iffin you keeps takin' in all dem urchins, you will work yerself to deaf!"

"I have to help them, Dembi. God has called me to help them. I must obey. Besides," she said, hanging a holey sock on the fragile rope strung between two trees, "I know what it's like to be all alone in this world. People like Mrs. Graham have been kind to me. Now it's my turn to do kindness for others."

Since Katy had moved into the barracks, she had worked tirelessly to bake for Mrs. Graham to earn money, and God had provided miraculously for her as she took in one child after another. Black children and white children, orphaned and on the streets of New York City as a result of disease or war or poverty, came to Katy's place for a warm meal and to learn the stories of the Bible.

Katy and New York City had survived the Revolutionary War, but it had left the city ravaged and partially destroyed. Because it was a seaport town, it was a city of immigrants and escaped slaves, which produced poverty on a monumental scale. There were a few organizations that took food and wood to people in need, but there was still much more need than people and resources to meet them. Katy knew she couldn't help all the children, but she wanted to help at least the ones the Lord equipped her to.

Katy raised money to support herself and her orphans by selling her cakes. She didn't have to stand on the streets selling her cakes as much as she had to in the beginning because she now had a long list of customers who ordered from her. Between caring for the children and running her makeshift bakery, the days flew by faster than she could count them.

"Now, listen," Dembi said, "I has important news! You gonna make the cakes for the Inauguration party for General George Washington! Mrs. Bethune say so!"

Katy smiled inwardly and sat down at her kitchen table. Perhaps General George Washington himself would make his way to New York and eat one of her cakes! Her Mama would be so proud. And so would John.

"Dembi, I have another surprise for you," Katy whispered.

"What you whispering foe? Yew afraid da fishes in da ocean gonna hear you?"

"I don't want anyone to know."

"Know what?"

"Mr. Ferguson has asked me to marry him," Katy put her hands over her mouth giggling.

"Pshaw, Katy, everyone done know'd he sweet on you and you sweet on him. We all been planning dat wedding well over a year now!"

"John says we can get married in October by Pastor Williams from the John Street Methodist Church. Except that, he says we can't do the vow "till death do us part,' even though we are free."

Dembi nodded. Free Africans and slaves living in the city were constantly at risk of being kidnapped in the night and sold to plantation owners in the south. So the slave vows did not include being together until death.

157

The days flew and soon Katy was married and busier than ever caring for her husband, running her bakery, and caring for and teaching the orphans in New York City. On Sundays she opened her doors to any children and families who wanted to come, and gave them meals and lessons. But New York City was changing, and soon opulent mansions were being rebuilt next to the old battery barracks. They didn't like seeing the poor coming and going from Katy's school. They decided to convert Katy's hard-earned shelter into a park. Katy was forced to move.

Katy and John found a humble house on Warren Street to rent. It had a wooden floor! Katy loved her wooden floor. No longer would she have to fight to keep the dust out of her baked goods! She was thankful for her new home. She felt like a queen.

But she worked until she was exhausted each day, and no matter how hard she pleaded for help with the children she cared for, help too often did not come.

"Mrs. Chapman, would you be able to come help me with the children?"

"Certainly not," she said, pointing her nose to the sky and walking away.

"Mr. Comstock, would you please help me teach the poor white children?"

"You will not catch me teaching those crackers[3]," he harrumphed, and stomped away.

"Katy, you are wasting your time. Those black orphans do not have the capacity to learn," people would say. But Katy knew better. She knew she was smart, and she knew the children she cared for were smart, too.

---

[3] Poor white children

Not everyone was unsympathetic, and Katy was not too shy to ask for donations of clothes, shoes, linens and eating utensils. Some of the church ladies would send flour and corn meal and sugar to help her with her baking. After all – it wasn't for her – it was for the children!

"Let the little children come to me," Katy would say to those she asked to help. "It's what Jesus would do. Then it's what we should do, too." And she would quote from Matthew 25:34-40:

'Come, ye blessed of my Father, inherit the kingdom prepared for you from the foundation of the world: For I was hungry, and ye gave me meat: I was thirsty, and ye gave me drink: I was a stranger, and ye took me in: Naked, and ye clothed me: I was sick, and ye visited me: I was in prison, and ye came unto me. Then shall the righteous answer him, saying, Lord, when saw we thee hungry, and fed thee? or thirsty, and gave thee drink? When saw we thee a stranger, and took thee in? or naked, and clothed thee? Or when saw we thee sick, or in prison, and came unto thee?

And the King shall answer and say unto them, Verily I say unto you, Inasmuch as ye have done it unto one of the least of these my brethren, ye have done it unto me.'"

Often on his way home from work, John would gather up orphans he would find hiding inside empty hogsheads or under carts on the docks where he worked. He would bring them home and Katy would clean them up, put a hearty meal in their tummies, and teach them about Jesus. Not all of them lived with her. She worked hard to find good homes for all of them or find apprenticeships for the older ones so they could learn a trade and learn to support themselves, but in her lifetime Katy was mother to over 48 children of all races from the streets.

Soon, John and Katy had a baby girl of their own. They named her Abigail. But New York City was becoming more dangerous every day. Katy couldn't help but worry sometimes what kind of world she had brought her daughter into. And now, not even a year later, she was with child again.

Slaves who had escaped from their owners in Haiti were making their way to New York. It wasn't long before white people began to fear black people – even people they had known for years – after hearing stories of what had happened in Haiti. Soon, New York passed laws and gave rewards for the capture of fugitive slaves, dead or alive. Katy constantly had to show her papers to prove she was free. Poor white people began to hunt fugitive slaves for the money. And one day, they went to the docks and murdered Katy's John.

"But he is a free man!" Katy cried. "He is just as free as any white man!"

After seven short happy years of marriage, Katy was a widow.

John Ferguson died bearing the name he gave himself. He was given a Christian funeral, but because of the color of his skin, Katy was not allowed to bury him in the city limits. In spite of that, Katy still took comfort in the African funeral rituals at the African Burial Grounds.

Katy had tenderly bathed and dressed John in his best clean clothes, as was customary for a Mende burial, and then wrapped him in a shroud. She fastened it tenderly with copper pins and cried as her friends placed him in a simple, pine coffin. They buried him facing east – toward Africa – and toward Jerusalem.

Not all the Mendes who were at the funeral were Christians like Katy. Some of the women performed the ancient Mende teijami ceremony, and sang the song that had been passed to them by their mothers:

Ah wakuh muh monuh kambay yah lee luh lay tambay

Ah wakuh muh monuh kambay yah lee luh lay kah

Ha suh wileego seehai yuh gbangah lilly

Ha suh wileego dwelin duh kwen

Ha suh willeego seehi yuh kwendaiyah

Everyone come together, let us work hard;

the grave is not yet finished; let his heart be perfectly at peace.

Everyone come together, let us work hard;

the grave is not yet finished; let his heart be at peace at once.

Sudden death commands everyone's attention,

like a firing gun.

Sudden death commands everyone's attention,

oh elders, oh heads of the family.

Sudden death commands everyone's attention,

like a distant drum beat.[4]


"There were so many folks at the funeral today, Dembi," Katy sobbed afterwards. "Many more than just the twelve the law man says can come."

"The law mans are askeered of our wailin' – they too afraid ta come arrest us," Dembi said, comforting Katy as she laid her head on her shoulder.

The mourners' wails could be heard all the way up Broadway at night and it spooked New Yorkers because they didn't understand. The outcries were the ritual wailings for the dead. They sang songs in their own languages and they sang hymns in English. Their elegies comforted them and comforted the family members who were hurting. In spite of

---

[4] Translation by Tazieff Koroma, Edward Benva and Joseph Opala

the laws forbidding slaves to hold funerals at night, doleful songs such as this Ashanti elegy were sung to bring comfort to the mourners.

> "I am an orphan, and when I recall the death of my father
> water falls from my eyes upon me.
> When I recall the death of my mother,
> water from my eyes falls upon me."

Sadly, a few months later, Katy lost the baby she carried in her womb. In 1803, her seven-year-old daughter, Abigail, was struck with Yellow Fever and died. Once again, Katy was alone without any family to care for or to comfort her. But she never turned her back on God. Instead, she gained strength from Him enough that even in the midst of all her pain, she found the strength to care for others. But she never married again.

By the year 1810, Katy's pastor invited Katy's Sunday School to the new church building on Murray street. But not everyone was keen on the idea.

"I'm warning you Reverend, if you bring those crackers and slave orphans into this church, we will pull our membership," people threatened.

"If they can't pay for a pew, they shouldn't be allowed to come in and dirty the premises," others would say.

But to his credit, the Reverend wanted Katy to bring the children to church on Sundays. People had never brought the poor and homeless to church before. But things were changing. Soon after, in 1818, Katy's church adopted an antislavery resolution. That same year, her old master finally publicly recorded her manumission.[5]

In 1830 the great evangelist Rev. Charles Finney preached over seventy sermons over a period of six months in the New York City area. There was a revival of Christian values and many of the colonists began to fight for the abolition of slavery. But there was also a group of people that wanted all black people to be sent back to Africa.

"Dembi, I am just as American as the white folks who want to send me back to Africa. I was born a free American. Why would I want to go back to Africa?"

**1839-1853**

Ironically, just as some people wanted to send black people back to Africa, the schooner *Amistad* arrived on America's shores carrying 44 of Katy's countrymen – Mendes – who had taken over the ship that had captured them.

Now those kidnapped Mendes were in jail in New London, Connecticut, awaiting trial. Katy prayed for them and their leader, Cinque, night and day. Black people who still had memories of their shackles came to Katy's house every Friday for Bible study and to pray for the captured Mendes. She prayed for the lawyers and every Mende by name. When the case went to the Supreme Court, she prayed for each judge by name, too: Taney, Story, Thompson, McLean, Wayne, Barbour, Catron, Baldwin and McKinley. She especially prayed for Baldwin because his mind wandered.

She prayed for the Mendes' lawyers, Roger Baldwin and former president John Quincy Adams.

"Those Mendes have families in Africa. Just like my home is America – their home is Africa, and that is where they belong. I'm going

---

[5] the formal act of freeing from slavery

163

to be praying night and day for those dear Mendes and their lawyers all by name," Katy assured Rev. Tappan.

When it came time for the Supreme Court trial, two of the judges who would have voted to put the Mendes into slavery were not there. The judge from Alabama did not come, and the judge from Virginia died! The Mendes were free! Rev. Lewis Tappan, a man who had gotten saved during Finney's revivals and founder of the "Friends of Amistad Africans Committee", was sure it was due to Katy's prayers.

While the Mendes had been in prison, they had learned about Christ. They boarded the *Gentleman* and returned to their homes in Africa as missionaries.

When Katy was seventy years old she finally had a "be-still" storefront bakery of her very own. Even at her age she worked tirelessly baking cakes to support her mission. She had held a Bible study on Fridays in her home for over thirty years, and she raised money for Bibles for slaves, even though she couldn't read the Bible herself. It was her dream for everyone to be able to learn to read and learn the Word of God.

On a Tuesday morning, Katy wasn't feeling herself so decided to visit the doctor. When she returned she went straight to bed but she kept getting worse. Katy knew it was nearing the time for her to go home to be with Jesus.

"Oh!" she said to a friend ministering to her, "what a good thing it is to have a hope in Jesus."

Katy whispered, "All is well," went to sleep and never woke up.

Rev. Lewis Tappan, wrote in her obituary:

"During her life, she had taken forty-eight children—twenty of them white children—some from the alms-house and others from their parents, and brought them up, or kept them till she could find places for them. She expended much money on their behalf and followed them with affectionate interest with her prayers. To my inquiry, "Have you laid up any property?" she quickly replied, "How could I, when I gave away all I earned?"

*September 30*, 1991

The archaeologists looked like tiny insects swarming around the gigantic cranes and tractors at the construction site at 290 Broadway in New York City. Workers had found graves of African slaves at the location where a new federal building was being built.

Stretching more than five city blocks, from Broadway beyond Lafayette Street to the east and from Chambers beyond Duane Street to the North, they were shocked to uncover the graves of 419 colonial slaves.

New Yorkers were astonished to learn their city had played such a big role in the practice of slavery in the United States. It was disquieting to realize that slaves had literally built New York City in the 1600's. During the Colonial Period, 41 percent of New York's households had slaves. Six percent of Philadelphians owned slaves and in Boston only two percent owned them. New York had the second largest enslaved population at the time of the American Revolution. Only Charleston, South Carolina had more slaves than New York City.

*October 4*, 2003

It was time to give the exhumed slave remains at the construction site a proper burial. They had been studied, photographed and cataloged, giving scholars a clearer picture of what life was like for the slaves during colonial times. Buttons, beads and pins found at the sties had given historians clues to their culture, religions and daily life.

On October 3, 2003, thousands of people from all backgrounds gathered on the streets of New York to watch the funeral procession for the 416 slaves wind its way to their graves at the African Burial Grounds. For over 200 years, other parts of the five acre burial ground, where an estimated 20,000 Africans were buried, had been ignored as streets and parking lots were constructed over their graves. Today, they were being honored and remembered so that future generations will remember them, too.

During the ceremony for the Rites of Ancestral Return, young and old alike learned more about what it meant to be a slave. At the very spot of the colonial slave market, South and Wall Street, during the arrival ceremony, New York Mayor Michael Bloomberg said:

"It's a painful landmark, a reminder of our city's portion in what the poet Langston Hughes called 'the American heartbreak'" he said. "Once the African-American residents of our city were bought and sold on this very spot. So it is fitting that here and now we reverently receive the earthly remains of some of them. As Mayor of New York, I welcome them home."

At 1:00 PM the next day, the remains were again laid to rest in beautifully carved coffins at the African Burial Grounds memorial site.

*February 27, 2006*

On the 27th day of February, 2006, President George W. Bush designated the African Burial Ground a national monument. Now generations of children and their families will be able to learn the truth about slavery in colonial times. Katy Ferguson, who gave her life to the teaching and betterment of children, would be pleased. Her loved ones, and the loved ones of many others, once ignored, were now given the dignity of recognition. At one time they lived, breathed, and helped build a great and thriving nation.

The African Slave Trade brought 40,000 ships across the ocean.

Slave traders captured and forced twelve million Africans to be enslaved in the Americas. More than 80 slaves per day for 400 years were made to suffer the bondage and abuse of being owned by another person. It was the largest forced migration in world history.

Slavery is indeed an American heartbreak, but recognition of these individuals helps to heal and build a bridge between the races – just as Katy did. Katy didn't hold grudges. She forgave her captors and prayed for her enemies. She saw problems and worked hard to solve them. To her credit, Catherine Ferguson, America's first Sunday School teacher, still teaches us today. We need only to listen.

"But I say unto you which hear, Love your enemies, do good to them which hate you."

Luke 6:27

*About the author:*

Karla Akins has been married to her husband, Eddie, pastor of Christian Fellowship Church in North Manchester, Indiana, for nearly 25 years. She is mother (and mother-in-love) to Melissa and her husband Brent; Jesse and his wife, Kara; Noah, 16, and Isaiah and Isaac,  11. She enjoys riding her motorcycle alongside her husband and taking pictures of her travels. Karla has homeschooled for nearly 20 years and continues to homeschool her three youngest boys and other students at her cottage school. You can read more about Karla's adventures in life and learning at http://homeschoolblogger.com/karlaakins.

*To my husband John and to our three children who have given value to whatever else I may accomplish in this life. And, to the women who have worked and suffered through the ages so we may all enjoy the privileges we have today.*

AUTHOR'S NOTE: Lucretia Mott never held a political office because women were not allowed to participate in the political system in her lifetime. However, her persistence in working for the rights of all people – for the freedom of enslaved African Americans and for the rights of all women to vote – made her an inspiration to those who knew her, knew of her, and for those who came after.

# Lucretia Mott

Equality for All

1793 - 1880

*by Judith Geary*

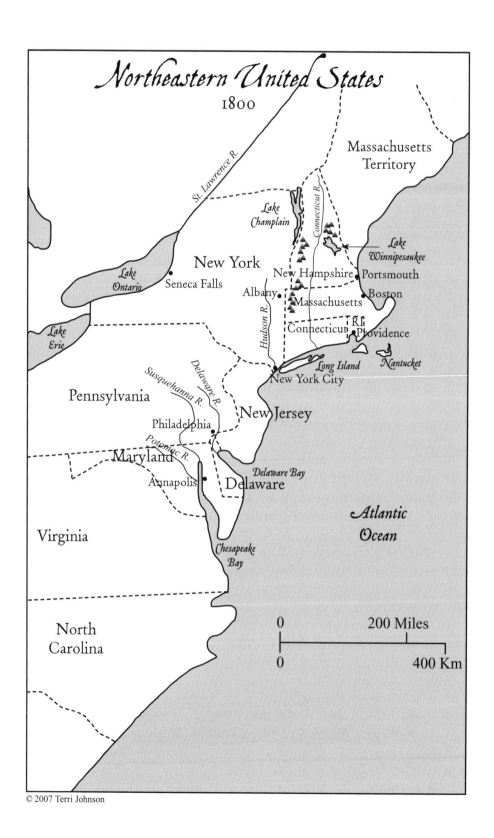

# Northeastern United States
## 1800

Massachusetts
Territory

St. Lawrence R.

Lake
Champlain

Connecticut R.

Lake
Winnipesaukee

New York

New Hampshire  Portsmouth

Seneca Falls

Albany  Massachusetts  Boston

Lake
Ontario

Hudson R.

Connecticut  R.I.  Providence

Lake
Erie

Long Island  Nantucket

New York City

Pennsylvania

Susquehanna R.

Delaware R.

New Jersey

Philadelphia

Potomac R.

Maryland

Annapolis  Delaware

Delaware Bay

Virginia

Atlantic
Ocean

Chesapeake
Bay

North
Carolina

0          200 Miles

0                  400 Km

# VII

## Lucretia Mott

### Equality for All

*by Judith Geary*

*July,* 1804

"But Mama," Lucretia protested. "I would not leave thee here alone. Thee is not strong yet."

"Nonsense." Anna Coffin cradled Lydia, her newest baby, only days old, as she sat propped up with pillows in bed in the borning room, the sunny bedroom off the kitchen reserved for sickness and recovering from births. "Aunt Phoebe and Cousin Mary Hussey will be here any time. And Sarah will be company for me until they get here."

"Sarah cannot help thee." Lucretia glanced at her older sister who was sitting in the floor in the sunshine, surrounded by alphabet blocks. Poor Sarah, though the oldest Coffin daughter at 13, was not as able as other children. A crash sounded from the front room, followed by a wail, and Lucretia whirled to answer it. "And I surely cannot leave the children here. Mary! Eliza! Thomas! What have you done?"

Four-year-old Mary sat on the floor of the front parlor. Honey-colored oil was splashed on the front of her apron and was spreading on the pine boards of the floor around her. Eliza, nine, comforted her, murmuring softly, and examined her palms for cuts. Thomas, six, picked at the blue glass fragments embedded in the thick whale oil.

"Oh, Mary, what am I to do with thee?" Lucretia scolded as she worked her way to the scene of the disaster, picking her way through the trunks and barrels stacked in the narrow room. "That was Mama's favorite lamp. Eliza, get some rags from the kitchen. Thomas, be careful. Do not cut thyself."

The bell over the door rang as Aunt Phoebe Hussey came in, followed by her own daughter Mary. Eliza escaped to the kitchen.

"Look! Thomas had an accident!" Mary Hussey pointed.

"I did not!" Thomas protested. He clutched the pewter collar from the broken whale oil lamp in one hand, the oil-soaked wick leaving a smudge on the front of his trousers. On the undyed lindsey woolsey, the oil stain did look suspiciously like he'd wet himself.

"Here. Give me those trousers." Aunt Phoebe was already unbuttoning the flap at Thomas' waist. "Does thee have another pair? Mary," she said to her daughter, "Look in the kitchen for a jug of vinegar. I declare, I should have come over early this morning; just look at this mess."

"I care for these children every day, Aunt Phoebe." Lucretia was examining the trunks scattered about the room, looking for the one where she'd packed Thomas' clothes. "We'll get the stain out of the floor before your rugs come in."

"Lucretia long tongue," Mama's gentle rebuke floated from the borning room. "Is Mary all right? Did she cut herself?"

Lucretia gathered her manners and told Aunt Phoebe she was

sorry and she would try to do better. She found a fresh apron for little Mary and clean trousers for Thomas, carefully locked the trunk again and placed the ring of keys in her pocket. She took Mary's hand and led her through the kitchen to her mother's temporary resting place. "See, Mama. Mary is well. Though we are truly sorry about thy lamp. It was the blue one, thy favorite, I fear."

"It was naught but a thing," Mama reached out to stroke a tear from Mary's cheek. "How can I grieve for things when we have thy papa home safe and the rest of us healthy? I confess, I do wonder when thy papa will return from the mainland. This disorder cannot be sorted out until our things are moved to the new house."

"Yes, I am persuaded Aunt Phoebe Hussey hopes to have us out from under foot and her own things in place as soon as may be."

"I'm afraid thy long tongue will be thy trouble all thy days." Mama could not but smile at her daughter even as she scolded.

"I am sorry, Mama, but Aunt Phoebe ..."

"Has been wonderful help in getting us all ready to move to the continent. I can only be glad that her husband – may his soul rest in the light – left her well fixed enough to buy this house. It will be a wonderful place for Mary Hussey to grow up."

Lucretia bent to kiss baby Lydia so her mother wouldn't see the face she made.

Mama was not fooled. "Poor Mary must grow up without her father. We must be very thankful that thy papa was returned to us after so long."

"Yes, Mama. I am thankful." Lucretia had to struggle to be good. It always seemed so much easier for Eliza. Even Thomas didn't have the trouble she did. "Shall I take the children and go find Papa?"

"Leave little Mary with me; she can help Sarah with her letters."

Lucretia started off up Fair Street toward Nantucket harbor, Thomas on one hand and Eliza following behind. Cousin Mary Hussey, also Eliza's age, caught up with Eliza. Lucretia stopped her. "Thee must go to help thy mother."

She had no wish to be unkind to her orphaned cousin, but Mary Hussey was sometimes difficult, and Lucretia had her own troubles.

Shells crunched under their shoes as the three children walked along. Lucretia gazed around her, determined to remember every detail of her home. The salt-weathered wood of the houses glowed like silver in the midday light. She knew each of the people who lived in these houses, was related to most of them. No children played outside. They were all in school. The Coffin children would have been too, but they were leaving soon for Boston.

As Lucretia led her charges onto the cobbled main street, they passed the one spot on the island that made Lucretia shudder in disgust. The whipping post. She had seen it used only once, but the memory still angered her. Someday she would find a way to abolish such things. No one aught to be shamed in that way, no matter what their crime. She quickened her steps, then stopped. Eliza collided with her back and whimpered.

"Eliza? What is it? Is thee hurt?" Lucretia turned.

"Why must we move to Boston!" Eliza wailed.

"Does thee want Papa to go back to sea?" Lucretia asked. "The last time, we thought we had lost him forever – as poor Cousin Mary's papa was lost."

On his last voyage, their father had been gone for over two years, and everyone had feared he would not return. After years of sailing on

174

other men's ships, Thomas Coffin had scraped together the money to buy his own ship, the Trial, to trade with China. Lucretia's mother, Anna, was left to manage the household.

As she often did when her husband was away at sea, Anna opened a little shop in the front parlor, the long narrow room with windows that opened onto Fair Street. When her mother had to go to "the continent" as the islanders called the mainland, Lucretia, then ten years old, took care of the other children, with the help of her grandmother and aunt.

When Thomas finally returned, he told the story of his ship being seized by a Spanish man-of-war and held in Chile. After many months, he had finally given up trying to win her back in court and had walked across the Andes to Brazil to find a ship to bring him home. None of the messages he sent had reached them. He came home with a knowledge of the Spanish language and a respect for the Catholic people, which he passed on to his children.

"But why can't Papa just stay here?"

Lucretia sighed. She hated to leave her beloved Nantucket as much as Eliza did, but Lucretia had trained herself, or at least she was trying to train herself, to answer the call of duty rather than what she wanted herself. "Papa says his new business takes him to the continent."

"But must we go to Boston?" Eliza wiped her eyes. "'Tis not safe there. Mary Dyer was hanged on Boston Common for being a Quaker. What will happen to us?"

Before Lucretia could answer, the shadow of a man in a broad-brimmed hat loomed over them.

"Buenos dias, Papa," young Thomas crowed.

"Buenos dias, Thomas." Papa squatted to speak to them. "Muy bien. What else has thee learned to recite?"

Thomas put his finger in the air. "Mary Dyer was hanged on Boston Common.... Papa, who was Mary Dyer? Do we know her? Who hanged her?"

Eliza took hold of their father's hand. "Please, Papa, do we have to move to Boston? I want to stay here."

"Lucretia? What stories hast thee been telling to frighten thy brother and sister?"

"Not I, Papa. Truly. Though, in truth, I don't want to leave Nantucket either. It can't be this beautiful anywhere on the continent. We learned about Mary Dyer in school – at least Eliza and I did. I expect the boys did as well."

Lucretia and the other Quaker children, from the age of four, attended a school attached to the Friends meeting house. The boys sat with the school master and the girls with the school mistress, but they used the same books and learned many of the same lessons. Papa pushed his broad-brimmed hat back from his face. "So, what did thee learn about Mary Dyer?"

Lucretia recited, "Mary Dyer was a Quaker martyr hanged in 1660 by the Puritans in Boston for refusing to give up her belief in the leadings of Christ as the inward teacher."

"In 1660!" Papa smiled. "That was almost 150 years ago. Well, God has softened the hearts of the people of Boston towards Quakers since then. At least, they welcome our money and our good commerce. Thee knows thy uncle Jesse and aunt Harriet already live in Boston. I must go and help Jesse in our business." He pinched Eliza's wet cheek. "And I want my family with me."

Boston's streets were very different from Nantucket Island. Instead of the low weathered cottages, swept by ocean breezes, Boston's

176

tall buildings shut out the breeze and reflected the oppressive heat of July back into the air. Trees lining the streets provided some welcome shade, but also blocked the clear ocean light.

Lucretia was shocked at the dresses some of the women in Boston wore. They looked as if they had come out in their nightgowns tied up with ribbons. On Nantucket, even women who were not from Quaker families dressed simply, usually in skirts and waists of gray, with black bonnets and white shawls. Fashionable young women in Boston copied Paris styles, white short-sleeved gowns, belted high under the bustline, in imitation of Greek statues. They also carried parasols and wore ruffled shawls of flower-printed, lightweight fabrics.

Life in Boston was different in other ways as well. Nantucket was largely a women's society. In the Society of Friends, known as the Quakers, women had taken important roles since the society's beginnings in the 1600s. Women even traveled in the ministry. With the men away for months or years, whaling or engaged in trade, the women of Nantucket ran the shops and schools and set the pattern for the social gatherings. Fathers, when they were home, fitted into the pattern of the household as best they could. On the island, where she knew everyone she was likely to meet, Lucretia could go to the market, the wharves, or wherever she wanted.

In Boston, Lucretia's papa came home every evening. But his days were spent in a different world than the women and children of the Coffin household. He had an office in one of the huge counting houses on the waterfront. But the wharves were considered too dangerous for Lucretia and the other children. Gatherings in the evening might include Aunt Harriet and Uncle Jesse, but also some of "the world's people" who were not Quakers. The men gathered together to discuss their businesses after dinner, and the women sat in another room doing needlework, busy with talk of their children.

Boston was prospering, sending sailing ships all over the world. Thomas Coffin's business prospered along with the city. He and Anna had attended only grammar school, but he wanted the best education possible for all his children. When they first moved to Boston, the Coffin children attended a private school. But soon, their parents enrolled them in a public school so they wouldn't fall victim to "class pride." It also gave them another experience of the difference between the Quaker world and the world outside. In Boston public schools of the early 1800s, girls were only allowed in for two hours after the boys had left for the day. Still, Lucretia considered it a good experience. "It gave me a feeling of sympathy for the patient and struggling poor," she wrote later.

Lucretia and Eliza soon mastered the courses in the local grammar school, and their parents looked for opportunities for them to learn in an environment sheltered from "the world's people." They chose Nine Partners School in upstate New York.

For Lucretia, who at thirteen considered herself a young woman, and Eliza, eleven, it was almost like embarking on an ocean voyage. School was in session throughout the year and students did not expect to return home until they finished their studies. It could be two years before they would see their family again. But Lucretia had been separated before from people she loved, and she was excited about meeting young Quakers from other places.

Anna received a letter from the school with instructions for what to send with each girl: "one or two plain bonnets; one cloak, not silk; two stuff or gingham gowns suitable for the season, made plain; three or four long checked aprons; one pair of scissors and one paper of pins." Fancy clothing would be returned.

"The school building is very like a barn," Lucretia wrote home soon after they arrived. "It is near 100-feet-long and three stories high. The boys have their end of the building and we have ours, with our own classrooms and playground. We sleep on the top floor, each with our own little bed, in rows in an open room so we can share the companionship of our fellows. It is wonderfully simple as it should be, with no useless frills.

"I have become friends with Sarah Mott, whose grandfather is superintendent of the school. He is very kind and wise and like a grandfather to us all. Indeed, I have read a book he wrote, *Observations on Education.* In it, he speaks out against the use of the rod and in support of equal education for girls and boys. With such nurturance, I am confident Eliza and I will do well."

Whippings were not used at Nine Partners, but punishment could still be severe. A rumor went around that one of the younger boys had been locked in a closet without his supper for breaking a minor rule. Lucretia had become acquainted with the boy at meals and felt sorry for him. She decided that she and Eliza should do something to help.

"We cannot go to the boy's side," Eliza said. "The rules forbid it."

"No one will know but me and thee – and the Christ within."

"But if we're caught, we will be punished as well."

"Shhh! Everyone will be at the lecture after supper," Lucretia reasoned. "We have heard Elias Hicks speak in meeting, and he is an inspiring speaker. Everyone will be attending to him, and no one looking for us. And if we're caught and punished, we will bear it with good grace, knowing we have done what is right."

"Thee believes it is right to break the rules just because thee feels like it is?"

"Remember what Elizabeth Coggeshall said? We must listen for the 'inward monitor' and to obey its leading."

"I don't remember," Eliza protested. The Quaker minister from Newport had visited the meeting on Nantucket only once, when Eliza was five and Lucretia was seven. Afterward she sat with the children gathered around her and gave them their own simple message – a message Lucretia had taken to heart.

"But thee has quoted her enough times since," Eliza added.

"My inward monitor tells me that I must do this, and so I must. Thee must follow thy own leading, I suppose."

At dinner, both girls concealed buttered bread among the folds of their skirts. Afterward, when everyone else filed out to the nearby meeting house, they stayed behind. The two sides of the building were supposed to be completely separated, but doorways connected them. Fortunately for Lucretia and Eliza, the doorway they chose was not locked. They found the storage closet where the boy was imprisoned and slid the buttered bread under the door to him. A muffled thanks rewarded their effort.

They slipped up the stairs and into the darkened dormitory. Lucretia realized they were not alone. A bed near her own held a shape, just visible in the moonlight from the window. The bed was Sarah Mott's. Sarah was a good friend, but she was also the granddaughter of the school's superintendent. Lucretia realized she dreaded something else much more than being punished for breaking a rule.

What if Sarah discovered what they had done? Her friend would have to decide whether to report them to her grandfather. Lucretia valued the praise and good opinions of her teachers. She had spoken with confidence to Eliza about the importance of following the inward monitor. Now, she doubted her own words. They must wait in the hallway until the others returned and come in with everyone else. She started to shove Eliza back out the way they had come.

"What is thee about now?" Eliza said, far too loudly.

"Eliza?" The shape stirred and spoke with Sarah's voice. "Lucretia?"

"Sarah," Lucretia said. "If thee is not well, thee should sleep."

Sarah sat up in bed. "I was feeling sick at dinner, but I feel better now. Come talk with me. Was Elias Hicks edifying, as usual?"

"As usual," Lucretia said, sitting on her own bed and motioning for Eliza to sit next to her.

"I suppose everyone was excited about the holiday?"

The holiday? Lucretia turned to Eliza, but her sister was staring at the floor and her white cap reflected only the moonlight.

"Grandfather planned to announce a week's holiday next month. I know it's too far away for thee and Eliza to go home, so I'm allowed to invite you to spend the week with my family in Mamaroneck. I can share the beauty of Long Island Sound with you. Did he not tell everyone?"

"We ... we were not in the ..." Lucretia began. The idea of getting back to the ocean, the soaring gulls, the salt air, almost took her breath away.

"Yes," Eliza spoke up. "Lucretia felt a leading to come back here... perhaps she was worried when we didn't see thee."

Lucretia gasped at Eliza's lie, but was grateful nonetheless as excited voices from downstairs announced that the other girls were returning with news of the holiday.


Lucretia immediately liked Sarah Mott's parents and her brothers and sisters — especially her brother James, tall, blond and eighteen. Lucretia had glimpsed him before. He taught on the boys' end of the building. She didn't see much more of him during the brief visit, as she and Sarah helped Anna Mott in the kitchen, and James worked in the fields and in Uncle Richard Mott's mill. But Lucretia liked what she saw.

Lucretia resumed her studies with her usual diligence, and by 1808, at fifteen, she had completed all the courses Nine Partners offered. No formal graduation marked the day, consistent with the Quaker belief that one day is no more special or holy than the others. Lucretia, an impressive student, was offered a position as assistant to the head teacher, Deborah Rodgers. She accepted, but first returned home for a visit. In the two years she had been away at school, baby Lydia had died. A new baby, Martha, was there to become acquainted with.

Upon returning to Nine Partners, Lucretia settled into her duties. While writing a report one evening in the school office, she discovered something disturbing. She snatched up the account book from the desk and hurried to find Deborah, who was reading by lamplight in her room.

"Can this be true?" Lucretia laid the account book, none too gently, on the bed beside Deborah. "Can it be true that thee is paid only forty pounds a year, while the male teachers are paid over twice as much? Even James Mott, only twenty years old and not nearly thy equal in experience, is paid one hundred pounds a year. How can this be? It is so unfair!"

"It can be, because it is," Deborah replied gently. "How is it that thee is snooping in the account books?"

"I was not snooping," Lucretia replied. "The book was open. The figures are plain. Did the elder James Mott approve of this?"

James Mott senior had retired in Lucretia's absence, but there was no evidence of a recent change in the policy.

"James Mott served without pay at all, as a service to the school," Deborah said. "Please, Lucretia, I value my place here. I find teaching to be a reward in itself. I pray thee do not cause me trouble over this."

Lucretia did not know what to do. Even within her beloved Society of Friends, a woman was slighted because of her sex! That she herself was not paid other than room and board did not trouble her, for she was just an apprentice. She did not know what to do – so she did nothing. But she did not forget.

Lucretia did not blame James; he only benefited from an unfair system. Now that she was a teacher, they were often in each other's company – at meals, at meetings, and in a group of teachers studying French. James was a quiet soul. Lucretia Long Tongue said what she thought. James never seemed offended by what Lucretia said – indeed, he seemed to quietly approve.

After a year, Lucretia was offered a "pay raise" – free tuition for Eliza in addition to room and board – and she agreed to stay another year. In 1809, Thomas Coffin had purchased a factory in Philadelphia for the manufacture of cut nails, a new product of the Industrial Revolution. His business was prospering, and he wrote to Lucretia that she should come home. She no longer needed to work. Lucretia returned, but with a proposal. She asked that he take young James Mott in as a partner. The two had not stood before a meeting to declare their intentions, but they had an understanding and the blessings of both sets of parents.

Philadelphia was different from Boston in many ways. Most noticeable to Lucretia as she and her mother shopped, were the many Friends Meeting houses and the many people in Quaker plain dress on the streets. They quickly found a suitable dress for Lucretia's wedding, a lovely gown in pale gray.

James and Lucretia were married April 10, 1811 as part of the regular Friends meeting. The guests signed a parchment scroll beneath a copy of the wedding vows, a custom that is followed in Quaker weddings to this day.

Lucretia and James Mott were an oddly matched couple. He was tall, blond and quietly dignified. She was short, dark-haired and vivacious. Yet they were a team in ways that few couples of their era achieved.

Many difficult years followed their marriage. The war of 1812 led to the failure of Thomas Coffin's business. He died of typhus in 1815, leaving his family deeply in debt. Part of the debt was due to financial decisions Anna Coffin had argued against. Lucretia complained that it wasn't fair that women like her mother suffered for decisions in which they had no voice.

Everyone pitched in to support the family. Anna once again opened a little shop. Lucretia taught at a nearby meeting school. James tried a shop as well, but seemed to have no talent for merchandising and found a well-paying job at a bank in New York. This job would mean moving the family once again. Instead, Lucretia found James a job in Philadelphia and tactfully wrote to him, "I shall rest satisfied with thy better judgment, but I should not mind being thought changeable if I were thee." James had the good judgment to agree.

Lucretia's second child died in 1817, a beloved three-year-old named after his grandfather. She struggled to deal with the loss. When people tried to comfort her with platitudes about "God's will," she was polite, but inwardly rejected the idea. God's laws operated everywhere, she was certain, uniformly and fairly. It was ignorant to believe otherwise. Someday someone would discover what had caused the fever that killed her son and how to cure it. She read books on religion and the Bible, searching for answers.

Lucretia and James attended Twelfth Street Meeting, where James was clerk. Quakers meet in silent worship, waiting on the spirit of God to lead members to speak. The clerk opens and closes meeting, but is not given the same authority as a minister. Searching for answers during meeting, Lucretia found herself on her feet, speaking aloud her prayer for divine assistance. At first she was frightened, but the members encouraged her, and she found the experience easier and more satisfying. She was often led to speak about spiritual truths she discovered in her reading, and her sweet, earnest voice and clear, simple messages ministered to her listeners.

In 1821, Lucretia became a recorded minister in the Society of Friends, an honor rarely paid to a young woman in her twenties. Recorded ministers traveled and spoke to meetings outside their own. Lucretia had accompanied a woman minister on a trip to the South in 1818, and she was haunted by memories of slaves working in the fields or chained in gangs on the roads. She drew from these memories and from books she was reading for some of her messages. Those who wanted to abolish slavery were called "abolitionists."

James was a member of the Pennsylvania Abolition Society and was assigned to supervise a free school for black children. He and Lucretia decided they would not use anything produced with slave labor. These products included molasses, sugar, and cotton – even paper made with cotton rags. As James was a wholesale dealer in cotton, it meant he had to convert his dealership to wool. It was a risky business decision, but James made it work.

Some members of the Society of Friends worked hard to abolish slavery. Others worried that Quakers were becoming associated with the turmoil these "radicals" were causing in society. By 1827, the conflict had become so severe that the Philadelphia Yearly Meeting split. Both groups, of course, considered themselves the "true Society of Friends." The activists named themselves after Elias Hicks, a speaker both Lucretia and James knew and respected from his connection with Nine Partners School. Lucretia was distressed over the split, but found that she simply could not deny "the leadings of the spirit." She and James joined the Hicksite branch of the Quakers. At times they were almost too radical even for the Hicksite Friends, and more than once they were threatened with disownment.

In 1830 William Lloyd Garrison, a young journalist, visited the Motts. He had just spent seven weeks in prison as a result of a libel suit brought by a slave trader Garrison had written against. Garrison was far from repentant. His experience had only confirmed for him that "Slave Power" interests were in control of the country and must be resisted. The Motts often hosted reformers traveling in the area, but their friendship with Garrison was life-long.

Garrison started his own newspaper, *The Liberator*. In it, he called for immediate reforms, including freedom for slaves and more rights for women. When Garrison formed a national anti-slavery society, Lucretia Mott was invited to attend – though women were not actually asked to participate. She made a few suggestions from her seat in the balcony. Four days later, she joined with other women, black and white, and formed the Philadelphia Female Anti-Slavery Society.

Why could those who saw the injustice in one form of inequity not see it in all?

Lucretia joined with other reformers who shared her commitment to the twin causes of freedom for blacks and women. They faced opposition from inside the movement, hostility from outside, and indifference from the authorities in Philadelphia who were charged with guarding the safety of its citizens. In 1838, the Philadelphia hall where they met was burned to the ground. Still, they made slow progress. The next year Lucretia and other "Garrisonians" worked to give women full membership in the American Anti-Slavery Society. Those who opposed women's membership formed a separate society for men only.

The climax of the struggle for equality for women in the anti-slavery movement came in 1840. A World's Anti-Slavery Convention was called for that summer in London, England. Lucretia and James Mott were among those chosen as delegates. The group from Philadelphia reached Liverpool on May 27, and the Motts took a leisurely ten day tour on their way to London. Lucretia was most interested in the way people lived. At a cotton factory, women were paid half the wages of men, and a pin factory employed little girls.

When they reached London, they were told the women would not be accepted as delegates but must sit as onlookers. It was a week before the convention, and Lucretia hoped that reason would prevail. In spite of much arguing, the rule was not reversed.

When the meeting opened, the delegates were seated below the podium, and visitors were in the wings. The women were conducted to special seats "behind the bar," a railing separating the back of the hall from the front.

Seated with Lucretia was Elizabeth Cady Stanton, the wife of one of the delegates. Elizabeth had known of Lucretia Mott as a speaker and had admired her for that ability. Lucretia's grace under the stress of the convention, her witty and intelligent responses when challenged, and her kindness cemented their friendship. Both the Motts and the Stantons remained in Britain for several weeks after the convention, and Elizabeth and Lucretia used the opportunity to know each other better.

They were an odd pair of companions on the London street, heads together in intense conversation. Lucretia was tiny, like a chickadee in her gray dress, black bonnet and white shawl, becoming more birdlike as she aged. Elizabeth was an athletically healthy bride of 25 in a traveling outfit, her skirt shorter than was fashionable, revealing walking boots.

"How did you bear it?" Elizabeth said. "To have come all this way as a documented delegate to the convention, and to have your credentials refused?"

"I was well warned," Lucretia replied. "So I was prepared. But I do admit, I am surprised at how well my body has served me. Usually, my dyspepsia plagues me terribly when faced with conflict, but I seem to be able to eat practically anything in England without discomfort – though the shrimp for breakfast were a mistake."

"Perhaps it has something to do with the many skirmishes you've won in the larger battle. The gentleman from Jamaica at breakfast last week, Mr. Prescod, when he said it would lower the dignity and bring ridicule on the convention to have women speak. And you pointed out that the same arguments were used in Pennsylvania to exclude the colored from the meetings ..."

Lucretia chuckled. "But that if we yielded to such flimsy arguments, we might as well abandon the whole enterprise."

"The same with Mr. Culver's argument that women were constitutionally unfit to mingle with men – constitutionally unfit – indeed! I did not think Mr. Prescod's skin could become any darker."

"He was angry, to be sure, to have those same arguments applied to himself, but perhaps he will think on it later."

"Constitutionally unfit," Elizabeth repeated. "I can sit a horse or hike a trail as well as any man. At the academy, I not only won a prize for my mastery of Greek, I could throw a ball as well as any of the boys. In fact, I'm not entirely sure women are not constitutionally superior."

"I'd not make that claim, necessarily." Lucretia patted her companion's hand. "Only that there should be nothing preventing any human, male or female, black or white, exercising the liberties God has ordained for us all. It was gracious of William Garrison to sit with us rather than take his place among the delegates."

"Yes, Mr. Garrison's support did cement your reputation as "the lioness of the convention," Elizabeth said. "And they treated you very like a queen. So many made the trip down from the podium especially to introduce themselves to you. Even Mr. Clarkson himself came to call on you."

Thomas Clarkson, now a gray haired statesman, opened the meeting. For many of those present, Lucretia included, his writings had first ignited their fire of abolitionism, and it had been a moving moment.

"Hmmm. Flattering," Lucretia said. "But compliments are no substitute for rights denied. Did thee ask Thomas Clarkson for a lock of his hair as a memento?"

Elizabeth blushed. "I did not ... I prevailed upon Abby to share her lock with me. But I should be asking you for a memento. I do swear you are an entirely new revelation of woman. I shall take you as my model."

Lucretia replied gently, "Not me, my dear. I am already a grandmother. The fight will belong to the young women like thee. Follow no human model. Listen to the spirit of God within thee. Let that be thy own inward monitor and follow its leading."

"Is it because you are a Quaker that you feel such a leading with so much strength?" Elizabeth asked.

"Perhaps it's because I have read the writings of the early Friends." Lucretia looked down thoughtfully. "But I'm very sorry to say that some of our most determined opponents are from among the conservative Quakers of today. Yet, some of our strongest support comes from those who call themselves Unitarians or Baptists. I'm afraid thee must find thy own leading."

"I will try to do that, my dear friend." Elizabeth said. "And my leading is that we must have a convention of our own when we return to America. A convention particularly about women's rights."

And so they promised each other.

In the years following the London convention, Lucretia continued to speak out for reform. She visited the legislatures in Delaware, New Jersey and Pennsylvania, and addressed the Congress of the United States – always asking for stronger legislation against slavery. She visited President John Tyler in the same cause. She worked with others to create a new charity called The Northern Association for the Relief of Poor Women. She served on the Indian Committee of her Quaker organization and spoke against "civilizing" the Seneca Indians by trying to convert them to white man's ways.

Lucretia and James joined the New England Non-Resistance Society, exploring Christian principles of what is now called pacificism. They believed that the evils of slavery must be resisted, but that it must be done with truth and love, not violence. Few Quakers of the day agreed, even among the more liberal Hicksites.

In the summer of 1848, Lucretia and James visited Lucretia's sister Martha and her family in Auburn, NY. While they were there, Lucretia and Martha were invited to the home of Jane Hunt, one of a group of Quakers active in the abolitionist cause.

Lucretia asked that Elizabeth Cady Stanton, who had moved to nearby Seneca Falls, be included in the tea party. Eight years had passed since Elizabeth and Lucretia's vow to each other in London. Elizabeth's letters, rare though they were, told of her husband's law studies with Judge Cady, his admission to the bar as a lawyer, their moves and her growing family.

"I do so appreciate your inviting me," Elizabeth said to Jane Hunt, clasping her hands warmly when Lucretia introduced them. Already seated at a table in the front parlor were Lucretia's sister Martha and Mary Ann McClintock. Jane introduced Elizabeth to the other women. Martha offered her tea cakes and poured her a cup of tea.

Elizabeth noted that the other ladies were all dressed in simple Quaker gray. Also, the room around her, though spacious and comfortably arranged, was simply decorated with plain curtains and simple padded wooden chairs. Conservative Quakers the Stantons had visited in England sometimes had elaborately decorated homes and liveried servants. The host and hostess, wearing "the best, though plain" appeared gray birds in a colorful nest.

"Lucretia Mott tells us thee is active in the abolitionist cause," Mary Ann said, using Lucretia's whole name instead of a title, as was the Quaker custom. "We are pleased thee is able to join us, Elizabeth Stanton."

"Lucretia is very kind," Elizabeth said. "As much as I am in sympathy with the cause, I'm afraid my life has been taken up with other things. That's why I'm so grateful to be included today." She paused, unsure how, or whether, to continue. An encouraging nod and a pat on the arm from Lucretia brought tears. "I've been so very isolated here – so very lonely."

The other women murmured encouragement, but Elizabeth quickly took herself in hand. "I'm sorry. That was rude." Elizabeth sipped her tea and nibbled a cake. "These are really wonderful, cakes,

Lucretia Mott

Mrs. Hunt. And I do believe this is strawberry jam."

"Martha made the cakes..." Jane Hunt began.

"From Lucretia's instructions," Martha said. "And she made the jam."

Elizabeth shook her head and smiled. "My dear Lucretia, is there anything you cannot do?"

"Many things, I'm afraid," Lucretia said. "But what of thee?"

"Pay me no mind," Elizabeth said. "Continue your conversation, and allow me the favor of listening to what you have been doing."

"I'm afraid our conversation would not be very uplifting," Lucretia said. "We are enmeshed in troubles with the more conservative factions in our own group. It sounds as though you may be led to speak to us."

"Led to speak?" Elizabeth was puzzled. She certainly didn't wish to burden these women with her discontent, kind though they seemed on first meeting.

"When one of our number is troubled about something," Lucretia explained, "a decision to be made, or something in their life that seems not right, it is common to call upon a few trusted members of the meeting to sit with them and allow them to speak their heart until clearness is reached. We would be pleased to act as thy clearness committee if thee is willing."

"I really have no wish to complain," Elizabeth began. "I do know that my life is so much better than those around me. It's just that when we lived in Boston, all my immediate friends were reformers. I had a new home with modern conveniences and well-trained servants.

"Here, our house is on the edge of town, the roads often muddy, and the only servants available are poorly trained. Mr. Stanton is so often away, and I have the entire responsibility for purchasing every article for daily use, getting our children to different schools, to dentists and the shoemaker, keeping half a dozen wardrobes in proper trim.

"We're surrounded by a settlement of farmers. It seems I'm always being called in to mediate their quarrels. At first it was because my boys had been throwing stones at their pigs or their cows. Of course, that required my utmost diplomacy. Now, if some drunken husband pounds his wife, I get a call.

"I do what I can to be a good influence. I lend newspapers to the men. I invite the children onto our grounds, give them fruit and our children's old toys and outgrown clothing.

"I do find it irksome to be called out in a dark night to prevent some drunken lout from disturbing his sleeping children or to minister to some poor mother in the pangs of maternity. Alas! Alas! Who can measure the mountains of sorrow and suffering endured by these terror-stricken women and children in the grip of poverty and vice!"

Elizabeth poured out her litany of troubles, with the encouragement of the other women, apologizing all the while for complaining when most women had it so much worse than she. Lucretia was thinking, and finally, spoke.

"As Ralph Waldo Emerson has said, thy discontent may be a healthy thing for all of us, dear Elizabeth. For it calls us to action."

The group decided to call a "Women's Rights Convention," and to do it right away. The vicar of a Wesleyan Chapel in Seneca Falls agreed to allow use of the building. They wrote the notice that evening and published it in the Seneca County Courier the next day, July 14, 1848. What is now known as the 1848 Women's Rights Convention was called for July 19-20. They had given themselves only five days to organize. Everything had to fall into place quickly, if the meeting were not to be a public and humiliating failure.

In addition to Lucretia Mott and Elizabeth Cady Stanton, speakers included Frederick Douglass, an escaped slave who had become an eloquent speaker, editor and national celebrity. James Mott, ever supportive, chaired one of the sessions. Over three hundred women and men attended the convention. One hundred – one-third of them men – signed the Declaration of Sentiments, modeled after the Declaration of Independence.

Lucretia Mott was an abolitionist, a radical, a pacifist, and a militant advocate of women's rights. What her mother had called her "long tongue" earned admiration and opposition from both sides of the polarizing issues of her day. In a day when women who could afford it had nursemaids, she cared for her own children. She worked as a teacher and volunteered her time as a traveling minister and an advocate for all those downtrodden in society. She searched for practical solutions for the problems of society. She was a century and more ahead of her time.

## Text from the Declaration of Sentiments

When, in the course of human events, it becomes necessary for one portion of the family of man to assume among the people of the earth a position different from that which they have hitherto occupied, but one to which the laws of nature and of nature's God entitle them, a decent respect to the opinions of mankind requires that they should declare the causes that impel them to such a course. We hold these truths to be self-evident: that all men and women are created equal; that they are endowed by their Creator with certain inalienable rights; that among these are life, liberty, and the pursuit of happiness; that to secure these rights governments are instituted, deriving their just powers from the consent of the governed. Whenever any form of government becomes destructive of these ends, it is the right of those who suffer from it to refuse allegiance to it, and to insist upon the institution of a new government, laying its foundation on such principles, and organizing its powers in such form, as to them shall seem most likely to effect their safety and happiness. Prudence, indeed, will dictate that governments long established should not be changed for light and transient causes; and accordingly all experience hath shown that mankind are more disposed to suffer, while evils are sufferable, than to right themselves by abolishing the forms to which they are accustomed. But when a long train of abuses and usurpations, pursuing invariably the same object, evinces a design to reduce them under absolute despotism, it is their duty to throw off such government, and to provide new guards for their future security. Such has been the patient sufferance of the women under this government, and such is now the necessity which constrains them to demand the equal station to which they are entitled. The history of mankind is a history of repeated injuries and usurpations on the part of man toward woman, having in direct object the establishment of an absolute tyranny over her. To prove this, let facts be submitted to a candid world. He has never permitted her to exercise her inalienable right to the elective franchise. He has compelled her to submit to laws, in the formation of which she had no voice. He has withheld from her rights which are given to the most ignorant and degraded men--both natives and foreigners. Having deprived her of this first right of a citizen, the elective franchise, thereby leaving her without representation in the halls of legislation, he has oppressed her on all sides. He has made her, if married, in the eye of the law, civilly dead. He has taken from her all right in property, even to the wages she earns. He has made her, morally, an irresponsible being, as she can commit many crimes with impunity, provided they be done in the presence of her husband. In the covenant of marriage, she is compelled to promise obedience to her husband, he becoming, to all intents and purposes, her master--the law giving him power to deprive her of her liberty, and to administer chastisement. He has so framed the laws of divorce, as to what shall be the proper causes, and in case of separation, to whom the guardianship of the children shall be given, as to be wholly regardless of the happiness of women--the law, in all cases, going upon a false supposition of the supremacy of man, and giving all power into his hands. After depriving her of all rights as a married woman, if single, and the owner of property, he has taxed her to support a government which recognizes her only when her property can be made profitable to it. He has monopolized nearly all the profitable employments, and from those she is permitted to follow, she receives but a scanty remuneration. He closes against her all the avenues to wealth and distinction which he considers most honorable to himself. As a teacher of theology, medicine, or law, she is not known. He has denied her the facilities for obtaining a thorough education, all colleges being closed against her. He allows her in church, as well as state, but a suborinate position, claiming apostolic authority for her exclusion from the ministry, and, with some exceptions, from any public participation in the affairs of the church. He has created a false public sentiment by giving to the world a different code of morals for men and women, by which moral delinquencies which exclude women from society, are not only tolerated, but deemed of little account in man. He has usurped the prerogative of Jehovah himself, claiming it as his right to assign for her a sphere of action, when that belongs to her conscience and to her God. He has endeavored, in every way that he could, to destroy her confidence in her own powers, to lessen her self-respect, and to make her willing to lead a dependent and abject life. Now, in view of this entire disfranchisement of one-half the people of this country, their social and religious degradation--in view of the unjust laws above mentioned, and because women do feel themselves aggrieved, oppressed, and fraudulently deprived of their most sacred rights, we insist that they have immediate admission to all the rights and privileges which belong to them as citizens of the United States.

*About the Author:*

Judith Gear discovered her love of historical fiction in writing classes with Orson Scott Card, who at the time was known only for his speculative fiction. Tapping history for tips on world building, she was hooked by the real thing.

Her background includes an MA in Education from George Peabody College and continued graduate work in writing, editing and literary criticism and a ten year involvement in a regional writers' group. Geary teaches at Appalachian State University and edits for High Country Publishers / Ingalls Publishing Group, Inc.

Her nonfiction publications include: A Quaker Commitment to Education," in *African American Education: A Proud Heritage, Cobblestone Magazine*, February, 1998, and numerous articles (available on the web) about ancient Rome. *GETORIX: The Eagle and The Bull*, A Celtic adventure in ancient Rome, is her first published novel. It was a finalist in the ForeWord Magazine Book of the Year Awards in both young adult fiction and historical fiction for adults.

For more information about ancient Rome, her current and future projects and curriculum to accompany the novel, visit the author's website: www.judithgeary.com.

*To Joshua, my oldest brother, for helping take care of me when I was little, and being a close friend, always there for me, as I grew older, sharing in my interests and dreams and always lending a listening ear; and for all he does for his family, and the love he shows, even when times are dif-fcult. And too, for his courage to stand up for those suffer-ing prejudices and in need of a voice.*

# Narcissa Whitman

## A Seed in Fertile Soil

### 1808 - 1847

*by Jennaya Dunlap*

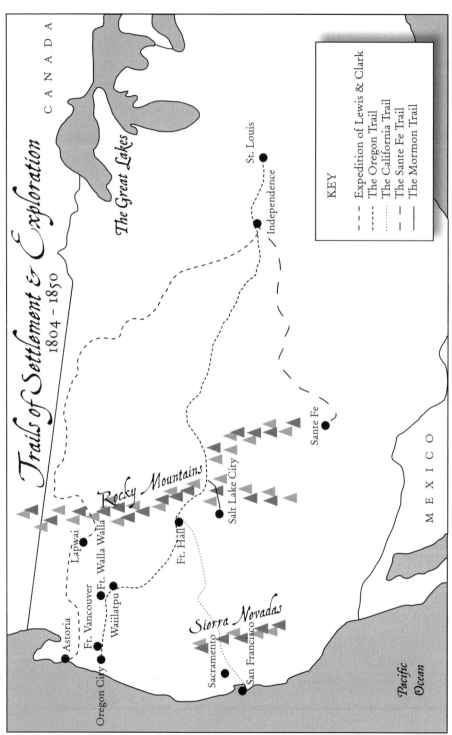

Trails of Settlement & Exploration
1804 – 1850

CANADA

The Great Lakes

St. Louis

Independence

MEXICO

Rocky Mountains

Sante Fe

Salt Lake City

Ft. Hall

Sierra Nevadas

LaPwai
Astoria
Ft. Walla Walla
Ft. Vancouver
Waiilatpu
Oregon City

Sacramento
San Francisco

Pacific
Ocean

KEY
– – –  Expedition of Lewis & Clark
· · · · ·  The Oregon Trail
· · · · · · ·  The California Trail
– –  The Sante Fe Trail
——  The Mormon Trail

© 2007 Terri Johnson

# VIII
# Narcissa Whitman

## A Seed in Fertile Soil

### by Jennaya Dunlap

*July, 1836, on the Oregon Trail*

"Arise! Arise!" A hunter called these words as the first streaks of dawn brightened the eastern sky. Immediately the mules, picketed together inside the huge circle of wagons, began to bray in anticipation of feeding time.

Narcissa pushed back her warm quilt and sat up, forcing open her tired eyes. She stood up and hurried to join her husband, loosing the hungry horses and filling their troughs with grain. The Fur Company men did the same with the pack mules, hurrying to get to breakfast before the sun came up.

Narcissa stepped quickly back outside the ring of wagons, kneeling by the dying campfire outside the tent to hastily prepare breakfast. Eliza Spalding bustled about beside her, setting out the tin dishes and heavy metal eating utensils. When the men joined them in the tent by their wagon, they had already set the food on the India-rubber cloth spread on the soft ground.

"And now for the chairs," Marcus said merrily, distributing blankets and boxes of various sizes from the baggage. "And here, Narcissa, is yours." He placed a box on the ground, offering her the seat with the same graceful air as if they were eating at home, sitting around a real table.

With great appetite they ate their meal of buffalo meat and bread, and washed it down with hot tea and milk from the four cows. Marcus led them in worship as they finished. He read several chapters from the Bible and prayed for their safety on the part of the journey that lay ahead.

While the men hitched the horses to the wagons, the women washed and repacked the dishes. Narcissa dried the dishes on an apron, having no clean dish rag. While Eliza packed them, she cleared away the remains of the morning breakfast and folded the tablecloth.

The eastern horizon was now aglow with brilliant colors, lighting the landscape ahead. Narcissa stood up and brushed her hand through her grimy hair. It had been months since it had last been washed, but there was no time to lose on such trivial matters.

While Marcus finished hitching the team, she took a moment to watch the sun rise. Two years ago she would never have believed she would be somewhere in the wilderness of the West on her way to a new land. Marcus reminded her often that she and Eliza Spalding were the first white women ever to venture this far west of St. Louis—the first to dare the dangerous journey on the Oregon Trail.

Two years ago was when they had first applied to start the new mission among the Cayuse Indians in Oregon Territory, and they had been accepted only several months ago. It would be a difficult task, and they would have almost no one to help them, but both Narcissa and

Marcus were determined to make it work.

"We must catch up," Marcus called, swinging up into the wagon seat. He helped Narcissa over the side. She had just settled in her seat by Marcus' side when the horses started, pulling the wagon forward with a jolt.

The Fur Company wagons moved into line. The pack mules were in the front where the captain and pilot were waiting. They began to move forward, slowly widening the gap between the missionaries' wagons and their own.

After crossing the Missouri river by steamboat, they had joined a company of seventy fur traders who were also on their way to Oregon. They were glad for the protection this gave them against Indian raids.

Narcissa sometimes rode in the wagon, but much of the time she rode on horseback beside it with Eliza as her companion. She enjoyed the view of the prairie and later the higher country, drinking in the natural beauty of God's creation. Sometimes herds of buffalo passed them, and the hunters stopped to shoot a few for provisions.

Her life was simple and the scenery changed each day. She was content to travel this way, taking each day as it came. But trouble was not long in catching up with them. The Platte River crossing was exhausting, because they could take only a little across in one load. By the time they had taken the last load over the river, Marcus had nearly collapsed, swimming though he was with the assistance of one canoe. Mr. Spalding fell sick, but they had no time to lose, for the Fur Company wagons were already four days journey ahead.

They stayed the night with missionaries among the Pawnee Indians, kneeling in prayer to ask for guidance. At last they decided to simply journey on as far as they could, with the help of one of the missionaries as a guide. They caught up before the company had reached the Pawnee villages beyond the Loup fork.

On a beautiful day in July, the wagons curved around a bend and came in sight of Horse Creek in the Green River Valley of Wyoming. Narcissa held her breath at the beauty of the land around the river. It was green with lush grass, and shade trees dotted the creek banks and were gathered in clumps among the rolling hills.

The Fur Company wagons slowly stopped. Narcissa saw large groups of Indians, both men and women, gathering about them and making signs of friendship and goodwill. She turned and looked questioningly at Marcus.

"These are Nez Perce and Flathead Indians," Marcus explained. "They've gathered by the river to meet with the fur traders at a rendezvous point. I met them last year, but there are more this time. They promised to help with the mission."

They pressed close and curiously observed the cattle, the wagons, and especially the white women.

Narcissa jumped down from her horse. Immediately the Indian women surrounded her and Eliza, showering them with kisses and shaking their hands one by one. Narcissa's heart welled with joy and she felt greatly moved by the unexpected affections of the native women.

The Indians sat down in the midst of their circle on the ground. They stared with delight at the white women, giving them warm words of welcome. One chief, who had met them somewhat earlier in their journey, pushed his way to the center of the circle with his wife at his side.

He introduced her to the two women, and again they shook hands and exchanged kisses with the woman. "My people like the two white squaws that have come among us," the chief told them with a smile. "They like you very much. We thank God that you have come here to us."

Narcissa Whitman

Now he spoke to Marcus. "When you come here one summer ago, I promise you that you will not want for food when you come back. Now you are back and I keep my promise to you."

Another chief offered them a horse, to replace one that they had lost along the way. "This is my gift to you," he told them. "We are glad you have come to this valley, so I give this to you and you have no need to give me presents in return."

They stayed with the Indians at the rendezvous point for more than a week before continuing on their way. Loaded with fresh supplies, they traveled with a Hudson Bay caravan, who were to guide them to Walla Walla in Oregon Territory.

It was another month before they reached the Walla Walla River, on August 31, exhausted from crossing the Blue Mountains. The next morning they set out for the fort in Walla Walla, invigorated by the prospect of being so near their destination.

With renewed energy they hurried forward. Even the animals seemed to sense that they were near the end of the journey, for they galloped the rest of the afternoon. They were received hospitably when they arrived at the fort, and were given comfortable beds in which to rest after their travels.

They would need to arrange with the Cayuse Indians about the location for the mission, but the Indians were away on a summer hunt. The Whitmans and Spaldings traveled by boat to Fort Vancouver for a visit. Narcissa delighted in the beautiful countryside of the northwest.

The men returned to Oregon to build the two missions, one in Waiilatpu among the Cayuse Indians by the Walla Walla River, and one in Lapwai along the Clearwater River. The Whitmans were to live at the Waiilatpu mission, while the Spaldings were to take up residence at the mission in Lapwai.

It was late in December when Narcissa arrived at the new mission on horseback, along with her husband. The sun was setting, casting a dusky glow over the hills around the peninsula of the river where the mission house was located.

The house and wooden floor inside smelled of new timber, and the windows and doors were covered with blankets. A warm fire was already crackling in the new fireplace. Narcissa sat down by the fire and looked around contentedly at her new surroundings.

"We have no furniture, and nothing to make tables or beds with yet," Marcus told her, coming in after tying up the horses. "The boards for the house had to be sawn by hand, so we had no extra time."

Narcissa sighed happily. "It's nice just to be here, to hear the river and look out at the hills beyond. This land will be so rich for farming and the hills are covered with good grass for the animals." She gazed out the doorway at the sky where the stars were just beginning to appear. "My mother and father started out with as little, or perhaps less than we have."

"Just think, she's the first white child to be born West of the Rocky Mountains." Marcus leaned over Narcissa's shoulder to look at his newborn daughter. Narcissa had become pregnant on the journey west, and Alice Clarissa Whitman was born on March 14, 1837.

Narcissa smiled, gazing into the baby's sleepy face, and stroked her fuzzy head. It was hard to believe, but it was true. And already the Cayuse people loved the child as much as Marcus and Narcissa did.

Much had happened since they moved into the hastily built mission house. Narcissa shivered as she remembered their first winter at the mission. She and her husband had survived the long, freezing months only because the Indians and the Hudson Bay Company had provided them with food.

Narcissa looked out the window, at the lush, green field in the distance where her husband was working, teaching the Cayuse people to farm. At first they had been reluctant to learn, but gradually, when they saw Marcus' success, their interest in learning agriculture grew.

The Cayuse Indians were skilled hunters and horse breeders, and more warlike than the Nez Perce, the tribe the Spaldings lived among. Though set in their ways, they had great curiosity about the new ways introduced by the Whitmans.

It was awhile before the Indians became interested in the Bible and Christianity, but slowly, as they listened to Marcus' preaching, more and more people wanted to become Christians.

Every moment of teaching the native children was precious to Narcissa. She enjoyed the work thoroughly, though only a small number of children came to the mission to learn. She taught them from the Bible as well as giving them other schooling.

A new mission house was being constructed nearby, with many more rooms than the small house where they now lived. (Emigrants on the Oregon Trail stopped at the mission to rest, and often the house was quite crowded.) Narcissa often walked to the building site to see the progress that had been made on the long T-shaped house.

One terrible day in June, 1839, tragedy struck. While Narcissa was preparing a lunch of cornbread and eggs, Little Alice slipped out of the house with her tin cup. Stepping out the door to follow her, Narcissa was stopped in her tracks by a terrified shriek coming from the river. Alice!

Her heart gripped with fear, Narcissa ran wildly down the path toward the river. "Marcus—come quick!" she cried out. By the time she reached the water, she had lost track of the place where Alice had fallen in.

Marcus and all the Indian men who were visiting at the mill jumped into the fast river and searched, while Narcissa waited in agony. Her mind refused to believe they wouldn't bring her precious child out of the water, safe and sound. Hours passed, but she kept up her vigil at the riverside, praying and waiting.

Marcus crawled to the shore, exhausted, and one by one the others gave up, but an old Cayuse man kept searching, moving further downstream. At dusk he emerged from the water with Alice in his arms, and she could see the horrible news on his stark face.

"Too late—we were too late." Before the old man finished his stricken words, Narcissa was on her way back up the path to the house, weeping with a grief that tore her apart inside. As the news spread to the Indians, the women flocked around her in the kitchen to comfort her, but she was inconsolable. For days afterward, she could hardly eat or sleep.

Narcissa didn't recover from her heartbreak for years. Although she was normally a social person, enjoying the task of caring for and entertaining the visitors who came to the mission, after Alice's death she became depressed and took more and more to her own room, where she poured out her grief in her writing.

Marcus' grief took a different turn. He grew quick-tempered, especially with Henry Spalding, his rival. Neither could agree on the how to go about the work with the Indians. Three other missionary families stayed with the Whitmans, and strained nerves and frustration led to quarrels among them. Narcissa couldn't bear to see the petty enmities that had sprung up in the mission.

*Waiilatpu Mission, near Walla Walla, Oregon; October, 1842*

Narcissa sat back in her chair, the load of worries and sorrows weighing heavily on her. She heard heavy steps outside and the door opened. Marcus came in quietly and she could see that he had bad news.

"What is it?" she asked, looking up as he sat down with a sigh.

"The letters I sent to the board, complaining about Henry Spalding... and all the other letters sent by other people here about the ongoing strife ... they've looked over them and they want to close the missions here and in Lapwai." Marcus buried his head in his hands. "They want us to return east, us and the Spaldings and a few of the other missionaries."

Narcissa listened to her husband's terrible news with a sinking heart. "Isn't there some way to save the mission?" In the darkness of the kitchen, she watched the embers of the fire dying down.

"It will be no use to send letters of appeal." Marcus' gaze was on the ground. "Even though we've solved our differences with the Spaldings the decision is final. It would take a year for a letter to reach them."

"But we can't just leave," Narcissa cried. "All our work will be wasted. The Cayuse people are finally becoming interested in the Gospel. And we've only just built the new mission...." In the silence that followed she could hear the winter birds calling from the river beyond the house.

A knock on the door made them both look up. Henry and Eliza Spalding had heard the news, and now they came from their mission to discuss what could be done about it. Together they tried to think of any idea possible to keep the missions open. But the situation seemed bleak.

Suddenly, Marcus leaned forward. "I know what can be done. I'll go to Boston personally and talk to the Prudential Committee of the mission board. I'm sure they'll listen to me. Also, we will know right away what their decision is."

"But, Marcus, the overland journey is too dangerous," Narcissa protested. "You'll be killed! Anything could happen to you!"

"We need you here," Henry Spalding told him. "The other missionaries have left and we're nearly without protection from Indian raids."

"It's the only way to save our mission," Marcus answered urgently. "Someone has to take the case there directly."

"But it's almost winter," Narcissa said. "How can you cross the mountains without a guide?"

At last they agreed reluctantly that it was their only choice. Marcus found an emigrant and an Indian guide to accompany him, and he set out on the long overland trip on October 3, 1842, a few days later. Narcissa watched at the door until he was out of sight over the hill, then sat heavily in her rocking chair. They had come so far—they couldn't give up now.

Narcissa was the only white woman left at the mission in Waiilatpu when Marcus left. The Spaldings had no room, so Marcus made arrangements before he left for her to go by wagon to Fort Walla Walla, leaving a hired man to stay at the mission.

Marcus succeeded in convincing the board in Boston to leave the missions open. When he returned, he helped a wagon train consisting of a thousand pioneers to cross the perilous Oregon Trail to the mission. It was a significant journey, and its success convinced many in the East to travel westward.

Narcissa returned from Fort Walla Walla shortly before he arrived at the mission, and threw herself into his arms with tears of joy when she heard the good news.

By 1844, fifty Indians were farming the land near the mission, and most of the Cayuse people owned herds of cattle. A sawmill had been built, with the help of emigrants staying through the winter. Marcus used his skills as a doctor to administer medicine to the sick in the Cayuse tribe. And more and more, the Whitmans found their time taken up by the emigrants passing through, train after train of wagons filled with exhausted families.

The Whitmans adopted three Indian children. Narcissa was happier now, with mothering responsibilities once again, though she often visited the grave of her lost daughter.

*October* 17, 1844

"Hurry with the dishes," Narcissa instructed nine-year-old Maryann, one of her adopted Indian daughters. "Today is going to be a busy day." She glanced out the window, her eyes resting on the grave of her poor child, and remembered the tragic story told by the young captain who had visited a few days ago.

Seven children, orphaned on the trail, now ragged and starved, with no one to care for them. Tears had come to her eyes at Captain Shaw's description of their terrible plight. He'd asked her to care for them for a few weeks, and she had managed to obtain Marcus' agreement, though he was reluctant.

The rumble of wagon wheels outside brought her back from her thoughts. Behind her, Captain Shaw put on his hat and headed for the door. "Your children have come—will you go out and see them?"

Throwing a shawl over her shoulders and tying her sunbonnet, she followed, with seven-year-old Helen, another of her adopted children, close behind. Halfway down the walk she paused, gripped by

212

the sight in front of her. A worn-down cart was stopped in the path, with a pair of oxen standing by, their heads drooping with exhaustion.

Two boys, bony thin and dressed in what could only be called rags, leaned against the sagging front of the cart, sobbing. The girls hung onto the side, their faces haunted by fear and misery. One girl held a baby, wrapped in a dirty blanket, while another supported the oldest girl, whose leg was bound in a ragged, makeshift cast.

Narcissa fought back tears as she made her way toward them. "Poor children," she whispered. "No wonder you cry." Wiping her eyes, she took charge of the situation. She gave quick directions to the weeping boys and one of her Indian helpers, to bring the few belongings remaining in the cart to the house.

"Come to the house, all of you," she told the girls. Helen grabbed the younger girls' hands and led them toward the door, but the girl with the broken leg clung to the cart with a frightened look. Narcissa took her arm and supported her, helping her up the path.

"The papoose is sick," the Indian woman gasped, lifting the baby's blanket as she took her from one of the girls.

"Get her inside, quickly," Narcissa told her, her heart sinking. "Poor child—this baby needs treatment immediately." Inside, she fed her hot broth in small spoonfuls, touching the child's thin arms with a sad sigh. Then, sinking into a chair, she gathered the children into her lap, as many as could fit, and the others crowded around her.

The door opened, and Marcus stood in the doorway, surprise on his face. He took off his hat and stared for a moment, and Narcissa couldn't help laughing. "They're your new children, Marcus. Come and meet them."

She watched, amused, as he sat down in a nearby chair, reaching out his arms toward one of the little girls. But she backed away and ran sobbing to the oldest sister, who had introduced herself with a shy smile as Katie.

"They'll get used to you in time, and you to them," Narcissa assured Marcus. "But my concern right now is for the baby—without proper care he may die."

"But—you're wanting to keep them?" Marcus looked at her wonderingly.

Narcissa nodded, lifting one of the girls into her lap. "They have nowhere else to go, and I'd love to have them here."

Marcus smiled. "If you want it, then I'm fine with them staying. I'll tell Captain Shaw."

Soon after the Sager children arrived, life at the mission settled into a comfortable routine. All week, Narcissa taught the children in the schoolroom, but in the afternoons she took them on walks in the beautiful, hilly countryside around the mission. In wintertime, the mission was crowded with Indian children who came to attend the school and stayed there until spring.

Sundays were quiet days of rest, spent in relaxing activities and studying the Bible. Narcissa gave each of her adopted children a subject to research from the Bible, and when Marcus came in for devotions, she had them present their research, one by one, followed by discussion. They read a Bible chapter together, taking turns so each could read a few verses and give their comments on them. On Sunday afternoons, Marcus left to hold a service for the Indians, and while he was gone, Narcissa and the children learned verses together and sang hymns.

Their lives were simple, yet happy and fulfilling. Everyone, including the boys, helped with the work, talking and joking together. The girls loved to help Narcissa in her flower garden, which she had planted years earlier with seeds she'd brought from the East.

The oldest Sager girl, Katie, became Narcissa's close friend and confidant, like a daughter of her own. They often talked for hours. Some of the loneliness since little Alice died faded. When Narcissa was sick, Katie stayed at her bedside as her constant companion.

Relations between the Whitmans and the Cayuse people were good. On one occasion, a band of Delaware Indians visited, and Marcus and Narcissa arranged a meal for them, with meat and cornmeal mush, served in the big yard in front of the mission.

Meanwhile, more and more wagon trains passed through, stopping at the mission. Narcissa was always busy, serving large numbers of guests every night, but it was nice to socialize with others who had made the hard journey westward. She often thought back to her own journey, and it felt incredible to think that she and Eliza had been the first white women to attempt it.

One day, a large wagon train came through, with many emigrants, mostly men. They milled about the kitchen that evening, talking and laughing, while waiting for their meal. When Narcissa was on her way to the table with a pot of cornmeal, a well-built man bumped into her, stepping on her foot. He slouched away without even an apology.

"How could someone be so rude?" Katie protested, coming up behind her with a look of shock. Her leg was better now, though she still limped a little.

Narcissa sighed, reaching for a pile of plates from the cupboard. "I'm just going to ignore it this time—it's important to keep on good terms with the emigrants."

"Mr. Whitman," the leader of the wagon train motioned for Marcus to join him in a corner. Sensing trouble, Narcissa strained to listen, pausing in the midst of her work. The man's voice was low, but she caught most of his words.

He was pointing to the man who had stepped on Narcissa's foot. "We can't take him any further on the trail—we've tried everything, but he refuses to stop his bad behavior. We brought him here in hopes that you'd take him in, maybe give him some work."

Uneasiness built in Narcissa's stomach, and she was glad when she saw Marcus hesitate. "We are already having conflict here, especially with the new Catholic mission moving in nearby," he was saying.

"If you can't take him, perhaps no one will," the man persisted. "He'll have to return by himself."

Narcissa had always been willing to accommodate the frequent guests who were dropped off at the mission to stay, because she hated to see anyone turned away. But this time she couldn't shake off the uneasy feeling inside—instead it grew steadily worse. Though still hesitant, to her alarm, Marcus seemed to be giving in..

"Marcus, please—I don't feel good about this," she took his arm and spoke in a low tone, though she had kept silent until now.

Marcus sighed, turning away. "I don't think we have much choice—perhaps he won't stay long." Frustrated, Narcissa turned back to her work, not without noticing a brief glare from the man in question.


### *Late* 1847

The man, whose name was Jo Lewis, stayed far longer than they had expected. In spite of her misgivings, Narcissa treated him with hospitality and kindness, but his morose attitude remained unchanged. He worked about the mill, but often slouched off in the company of a former French helper, also named Joseph, and sometimes both were gone for hours.

Meanwhile, troubles for the mission increased. Differences in doctrine between the Catholic and Protestant missions confused the

Indians, causing many arguments among them over who was right. When the cold nights of the fall came, a wagon train arrived full of emigrants sick with the measles.

Narcissa tried to keep them away from the children, but it was no use. First the children turned dangerously ill, and then one morning she herself woke up with a raging headache. It was all she could do to stay on her feet and care for household matters. That day, in mid-afternoon, one of her Indian friends ran into the kitchen, her face holding fright and alarm.

"Come quick—the people of my village are sick, and it's spreading fast," she gasped. Praying under her breath for God's help, Narcissa grabbed medicine and followed the woman out of the house.

It was the beginning of the worst nightmare she could imagine. She divided her days between caring for her own family and the emigrants at the mission and treating the Indians, who had no immunities to the illness. Before long, several of the Cayuse people were dying every day from measles.

Jo Lewis and the other Joseph were absent from the mission most of the time now, to Narcissa's relief. It would be hard to deal with their hostility on top of the measles epidemic. But when she mentioned this to Marcus, as he was packing clothes for a mission trip with Mr. Spalding, he gave her a grave look and left the house.

When he had been gone only a few days, the Sager children and the other children they had adopted grew sicker, until their lives were in danger. Weary and sick with fear, Narcissa sent Stickas, a Christian and a good friend from the Indians, with a message for Marcus, asking him to return immediately to help.

One day, she and an Indian woman stepped inside a high-roofed dear skin tent, medicine in hand, and Narcissa knelt by the side of an old woman who was covered in red spots and having trouble breathing. Suddenly, she heard a commotion outside the tent, and a man and woman rushed in, holding their sick child.

"You poisoned him," the man's face held terror and betrayal. "You told me you would save my son, but you gave him poison, and now he's dying."

Shock rushed over Narcissa, and she turned her gaze toward him with a gasp. "I gave your son medicine, to help him get well—I would never think of poisoning anyone."

"He grew worse when he took your medicine—what else could it be but poison?" After threatening her, the man led his weeping wife away, clinging to his child. Now the old woman opened her eyes wide in terror.

"Get away from me—don't give me any of your poison!" she cried out. Shaking, Narcissa tried to convince her it was only medicine, but to no avail. Ready to collapse, she rushed home in hopes that Marcus had returned—perhaps he could help. But the house was quiet except for the sick cries of the children.

Tossing the medicine bottles on the table, she pulled off her coat. "Mother, mother," Helen's rasping voice called to her from the bedroom. Suddenly the world seemed to spin out of control around her, and she grasped the table for support. How she reached Helen's bedside she didn't know, but she collapsed into it and lay still as the hours passed.

She was too sick and frightened by the accusations of the Indians to respond much when she heard Marcus' step in the kitchen. In a moment he was standing in the bedroom doorway, and she lifted her head to look at him.

Complete exhaustion showed in his eyes, and there was a heavy droop to his shoulders. He laid a hand on Helen's forehead and shook his head. "She's dying—if she doesn't get any better in a few hours, I fear—" His voice broke off and he sank into a chair.

All that evening, he was silent, and when Maryann came in with a bucket of water, he started forward, his hands shaking. Even when Helen's condition started to show signs of improvement and she was sleeping peacefully, his anxiety seemed to decrease very little. Finally, alarm building inside her, Narcissa sat up in bed and faced him.

"Marcus, tell me—what's the matter?" Dread came over her when he stood to see if the other children were asleep before answering. Did it have something to do with the accusations of poisoning, with the rising anger she had sensed?

"Narcissa, come—I must talk to you," he drew her by the arm toward the window, where storm clouds formed a barrier over the moon's light. Helping her into a chair, he sat down beside her. "When I left the lodge where Mr. Spalding and I were staying, Stickas came out and warned me that Jo Lewis and Joseph are spreading rumors, telling the Indians that we're poisoning them—killing them on purpose to give their land to the white people."

Narcissa clapped a hand over her mouth, horror washing over her as she remembered the anger, the confusion, on the Indians' faces that day. "But why? Why would he spread such lies? I always knew he didn't like us, but surely he wouldn't go that far."

Her voice trembled as she told him of her experiences that day. "They've always been so friendly—so open to our work. Why do they believe these lies so easily?"

Marcus' gaze was on the unswept floor. "Not all of them do. Many are still with us in their hearts. But the others—they're looking for an explanation, a reason why so many are dying. And they're already suspicious of us—it seems Jo Lewis has been spreading false rumors for months now, right under our noses."

Narcissa recalled with a sinking heart the heavy uneasiness she had felt that day when he arrived. *Why didn't I regard it? None of this would be happening if only we had stopped him then.*

"Stickas wants us to leave for a while," Marcus continued, and she snapped out of her thoughts, turning her attention to him. "If we left, we could wait out their anger—come back when the danger is over." He rose to his feet, shaking his head slowly. "Perhaps it's our only choice."


*Epilogue:*

The Whitmans made plans to move with the children to a safer place, and meanwhile continue to treat the Indians' illness, but it was too late. Early on the cold, gloomy day that followed, November 29, 1847, Jo Lewis and a band of angry Indians surrounded the mission and killed Narcissa and Marcus, along with the two Sager boys and many others who were at the mission, a total of fourteen. The Spaldings and those with them survived, because they were at a different mission. The Whitman mission was destroyed, and the remaining women and children there were taken hostage and held for ransom until other settlers were able to intervene and make arrangements for their release.

No one knows the motivations behind the massacre. Part of it was tied to Jo Lewis' lies, which he spread to avenge a general grudge he held for ill treatment in the east. Another part of it was connected with the huge number of white settlers passing through the area with little regard for the Indians, using up their natural food resources without payment or compensation.

The settlers in Oregon panicked when they heard about the massacre. They retaliated against all the Indians in the area, resulting in a war that lasted for several years, with much suffering on both sides. Meanwhile, all the missions in Oregon were closed, and that section of the Oregon Trail was abandoned.

Marcus and Narcissa Whitman made many mistakes, especially in their treatment of the Indians and failure to learn about their culture before trying to introduce them to a new way of life. But they did much good too, teaching the Cayuse agriculture and helping to educate them, as well as caring for them. Before the massacre, most Cayuse families owned cattle herds, given to them by the Whitmans. Narcissa and Marcus tried hard to stop the measles epidemic, and saved many lives with their work.

Both their overland journey and the mission they established helped to pave the way for future settlements in Oregon and California. In the decades following their deaths, the Westward movement grew rapidly, until large numbers of pioneers every year had the opportunity to start a new life in the land that had once been forbidding and dangerous for travelers.

*About the author:*

Jennaya Rose Dunlap wrote this story at
the age of 17. Jennaya is homeschooled and
the editor of a magazine for home schooled
girls, ages 8 to 18, Roses In God's Garden,
published by LightHome Ministries,
www.lighthome.net. She is also the author
of Against All Odds, a historical novel
set in World War II Poland under Nazi
occupation, published as a serial story in
her magazine. Jennaya enjoys writing and

researching, drawing, singing and horseback riding. She enjoys spending
time with her family on their acre beside a meadow with a mountain
view, in California. She graduated from high school this year and plans to
continue writing to publish.

*Illustrations*:

*About the Illustrator:*

Darla Dixon is a self-taught portrait artist and illustrator who works primarily in graphite pencil (black and white) and colored pencil. Darla also illustrated an earlier book in this series *What Really Happened During the Middle Ages* also published by Bramley Books. Darla maintains a busy schedule with her home-based art business, creating fine art pencil portraits based on her client's provided photographs. When she isn't drawing, Darla enjoys scrapbooking, reading, and writing in her blog. Darla and her husband Mark live in the Atlanta, Georgia area and have four children.

You can find out more about Darla and her artwork by visiting her website at www.darladixon.com or by calling 770-736-1584.